Andy Adams' Campfire Tales

Andy Adams'
CAMPFIRE TALES

Edited by WILSON M. HUDSON

Illustrations by Malcolm Thurgood

UNIVERSITY OF NEBRASKA PRESS
LINCOLN AND LONDON

Manufactured in the United States of America

First Bison Book printing: 1976

Most recent edition shown by the first digit below:
1 2 3 4 5 6 7 8 9 10

The introduction and text of the Bison Book edition are reproduced from the 1956 edition published by the University of Texas Press by arrangement with Wilson M. Hudson. The book first appeared under the title *Why the Chisholm Trail Forks and Other Tales of the Cattle Country.*

Library of Congress Cataloging in Publication Data

Adams, Andy, 1859–1935.
Andy Adams' Campfire Tales.

Reprint of the 1956 ed. published by University of Texas Press, Austin, under title: Why the Chisholm Trail forks, and other tales of the cattle country.
I. Title. II. Title: Campfire tales.
PZ3.A21An [PS3501.D2152] 813′.5′2 75–29131
ISBN 0–8032–0870–7
ISBN 0–8032–5835–6 pbk.

To Pleasant Middagh of Colorado Springs

Pleasant Middagh was one of the first friends Andy Adams made when he came to the Springs in 1894. With Jim Middagh, Harry Avery, and Arie Huyser, Pleas and Andy used to take month-long camping trips into the Flat Top Mountains. The last tale in this book begins with a description of the old route that they followed north from the railroad at Glenwood Springs to Trappers Lake and on to a favorite campsite at the foot of Sleepy Cat.

Preface to Bison Book Edition

This book was originally published by the University of Texas Press in 1956 under the title *Why the Chisholm Trail Forks and Other Tales of the Cattle Country*. After being out of print for several years it is now being republished by the University of Nebraska Press with a shorter and more descriptive title. I am very grateful to the Nebraska Press for making Andy Adams' tales readily available again.

It has been generally recognized that the oral tale has had a place in and an influence on American literature. In a recent article Walter Blair develops the view that the comic narrative modeled upon the oral tale has served as a "hardy continuum which survived changes for more than a century and a half" of American humor. ("'A Man's Voice, Speaking': A Continuum in American Humor," *Harvard English Studies*, 3 [1972], 185–204.) Blair distinguishes two kinds of comic narrative deriving from the oral tale. The framework story shows a storyteller in the process of relating a "traditional anecdote or one resembling it in substance and form." The writer describes the teller and the listeners and "reports" the teller's exact words. The mock oral tale is narrated directly by a pretended teller without authorial intervention. Though these two kinds of comic narrative have undergone changes, they have continued to be popular down to the present and their influence on American writers is still active. "I suggest," says Blair, "that the very nature of oral storytelling caused both skill and assiduity to come into play and that this was greatly to the advantage of the stye, the structuring, and the characterization in written humor."

The campfire tales of Andy Adams are included in Blair's selective roll of written narratives showing the influence of oral storytelling. What his article does for Andy's tales is to place them in the large perspective of American literary history. The tales in this collection all belong to the framework kind and most are comic in spirit though a few border on the tragic or sentimental. Andy allows for a wide range in campfire tales, as is indicated by the last sentence (p. 4) before Bill Durham begins his story about his experience with the vigilantes. It should be said here that Andy's storytellers prefer a rather low-keyed to a robust style of narration; theirs is a close approximation of the spoken language of their day and occupation, not an outlandish dialect overdone for the sake of effect. As Blair says, "Paradoxically, the effort becomes too evident when the writing is either too far from the vernacular style or too close to it." Andy escapes these extremes. A particularized discussion of diction and other matters follows in my introduction of 1956.

WILSON M. HUDSON

Austin, Texas
October 9, 1975

Contents

Andy Adams' Campfire Tales

Andy Adams' reputation depends almost entirely on *The Log of a Cowboy,* which is now widely acknowledged as the classic in its field. Such men as Eugene Manlove Rhodes, Charles M. Russell, Walter Prescott Webb, and J. Frank Dobie have given the *Log* high praise; they and others who know the West and Southwest have helped the book achieve its present standing. Its position seems secure. In a recent issue of the *New York Times Book Review* (May 6, 1956, p. 22) Mr. Hoffman Birney says confidently of the *Log,* "If there is such a thing as an all-time 'best' Western, that is it."

It has been said that the *Log* has won its place because of its inherently interesting subject, accurate and full depiction of trail driving, restrained and simple style, lifelike dialogue, fine humor, and freedom from exaggeration. In 1882 a band of men drive a herd of some three thousand cattle from Brownsville on the Mexican border to the Blackfoot Agency on the Canadian border; for five months, from April to September, they move over the Great Plains at an average of fifteen miles a day, meeting and overcoming such problems as dry drives, flooded rivers, quicksand, and stampedes; on the way they take a brief turn in frontier towns like Dodge City, Ogallala, and Frenchman's Ford. These men are joined together in the performance of a task which they successfully complete. They work, live, and eat together, and at night they tell stories around the fire. This plan gives unity and progression and it also makes possible the inclusion of episodic or incidental material. Into the framework of the *Log* Andy was able to fit his own memories of trail driving and life in the cattle country and also the memories of other men like him. There is so much truth in the *Log* and so little literary contrivance that it has often been taken for an autobiography instead of a novel.

One of the most delightful features of the *Log* is the inclusion of tales told by the cowboys at night. When Andy relates a story through Fox Quarternight or Joe Stallings, the sound of the human voice is heard and the language becomes freer and racier. Something in the talk around the campfire sets off the story, and at the end the other boys are ready with an apt comment or perhaps another story of the same kind. It is my belief that Andy was a master of the campfire tale, and the object of the present collection is to show to what extent and how skilfully he made use of this form. The only book of Andy's now in print is a shortened version of the *Log* prepared in 1927, and it omits four of the campfire tales. The original edition (1903) had twelve; they come first in this collection. Nine tales from *A Texas Matchmaker* (1904) follow, then eight from *The Outlet* (1905), and seventeen from *Cattle Brands* (1906). Beginning with "A Rise in the Price of Coffee," four tales are from an unpublished manuscript in the library of the State Historical Society of Colorado. The final tale comes from the *Breeder's Gazette* (XLVIII [1905], 1098, 1100). In all, there are fifty-one tales in this book. The titles have been supplied by the editor.

All the tales are told around a campfire, with the exception of "Alkaline Dust Ain't Snow." It was admitted because it was a live-voice story told by a cowboy to cowboys in a spirit of reminiscence. Since one tale suggests another, the number of tales exceeds the number of campfires. Fifty tales are told at twenty-one different campfires. The tales from the books are arranged according to the date of publication, and the tales from a given book follow the original order of presentation. The four previously unpublished tales follow the sequence of the manuscript in which they occur; they are told at one campfire—Andy put them together under the title "Mixed Brands." It seemed that "Cow Coroner for the Sap" should conclude the collection because it was the story of a man who had been a trail boss and who became claim agent for a railroad after the passing of the old trail days.

Though the tales could stand by themselves as complete literary units, something is to be gained from a knowledge of when, where, and how they happened to be told. For this reason, enough of what precedes and follows each tale is given to make clear the mood and circumstances of its telling. But not every tale has a forepiece or an afterpiece; sometimes a paragraph or a bit of conversation serving as a transition from one tale to another cannot be divided and must be placed with either the preceding or following tale. When a series of tales is told around one campfire, what comes before and after each of them provides a pleasing connection and adds to the enjoyment. Who would discard everything in the *Canterbury Tales* except the actual tales themselves? The first four tales from *A Texas Matchmaker,* beginning with "The Cat in the Jacal," are told while the pigeons shot by the hunters are being cooked in Dutch ovens resting on and covered with coals. Uncle Lance, who is supervising the cooking, has a look at the ovens between stories. The next two stories—"I'd Have Gambled My Life on Her" and "Miss Sallie of Shot-a-Buck Crossing"—are told at another campfire while the boys are baking wild turkeys coated with a thick mortar of clay.

When men gather around a fire at night in the open they begin to tell stories. The light of the flames holds their eyes and turns their thoughts to past happenings, both recent and remote. With the darkness at their backs and the flickering yellow light in their faces, they seem to be alone and yet listeners are close by if they care to talk. A case might be made for the campfire tale as a form of folk literature comparable to the ballad, but my discussion will deal with Andy's tales only. His storytellers lived at a certain time and place and they had tastes and conventions of their own. They were Westerners, or Southwesterners as they might be called, most of them being engaged in the raising, buying, and selling of cattle in the days of the open range. The great majority were ordinary cowboys. One tale is told by the owner of a herd on trail, George Carter, and another is told by an unnamed cattle buyer from Kansas City who has come out with Mr. Carter to look over the herd. The boys take a liking to the cattle buyer while he is talking, and when he finishes, the narrator expresses their opinion of him: "While he was a city man, he mixed with us with a certain freedom and abandon that was easy and natural." Eight stories from *Cattle Brands* are told by Texas Rangers, who are also out in the open around campfires. Unlike all the other tales in the collection except "Alkali Dust Ain't Snow," four of their tales are related in daylight, just after breakfast—they had been riding all night. The cowboys liked to sit around the fire and tell tales; sometimes they would stay up so late that they would have to be warned by someone in authority like Jim Flood or Uncle Lance to go to bed and get some rest.

There is a wide range in the subject matter of Andy's campfire tales. Speaking generally, he says, "The stories told may run from the sublime to the ridiculous, from a true incident to a base fabrication, or from a touching bit of pathos to the most vulgar vulgarity." Andy does not tell any of the vulgar kind, though most of the other varieties and extremes may be found in this collection. The only tale that might offend is "Good for Two Drinks," which is not for the squeamish. Incidentally, Andy himself, six feet three tall and 220 pounds in weight, would sometimes faint at the sight of his own blood. "Bibleback's Christmas Beef" and "Big Tom Plays Monte" have sentimental endings, and all of "Death of the Little Glassblower" is pathetic, perhaps too much so. Most of Andy's tales are told as true incidents and most of them have a strong element of humor. The taste of his Westerners runs to the true and the humorous tale. They do not want fiction or lies. "The Cat in the Jacal" is an old folktale involving the supernatural; to make it acceptable Andy has Scales present it as a dream brought on by too much drinking. After Waterwall finishes his story about Uncle Dave Hapfinger, Jack Splann tries to tell a story about the friendship of a lamb and a dog, but it is so "unreasonable" that nearly every statement is questioned. "Long before he had finished, Sponsilier checked his narrative and informed him that if he insisted on doling out fiction he must have some consideration for his listeners, and at least tell it within reason." Splann refuses to go on; he is unable or unwilling to make his story sound plausible.

Though the taste is for true incidents and the teller may take a prominent part in his story, he has to be careful not to seem boastful. In the forepiece to "Bogged to the Saddle Skirts in the Story" Parent, the cook, "began regaling us with personal experiences, in which it was evident that he would prove the hero." He is interrupted by a friendly scuffle between a pair of bunkies who are trying to make each other get a firebrand to light their pipes. Parent is offended and will not continue, so the boys are "spared listening to his self-laudation."

The boys do not want to hear an obvious fiction, nor do they want to have a sell palmed off on them, though they enjoy "selling" a tenderfoot. When Bull Durham is telling about his encounter with the vigilantes, he happens to use the law term *capias* and Quince Forrest interrupts him on the pretense that he wants to make a memorandum of the word so that he can use it too. In making this interruption Quince is violating an unwritten law that every storyteller is to have his say without distractions of any sort. After finishing his story, Bull gets even by drawing Quince on to tell about a stampede he was in the year before; just as Quince gets a good start all the other boys, who have been given the wink, fall back and cut loose with loud snores. Quince takes revenge at another campfire with his tale about the ox who stole a ride in a freight wagon. To begin with, the boys are not too anxious to hear his tale: "We all hoped that he would mount and ride out to the herd, for though he was a good storyteller and meaty with personal experiences, where he thought they would pass muster he was inclined to overcolor his statements." They regard him as "a cheerful, harmless liar." Quince manages to conceal the point of his story until the end, much to the disgust of the boys.

The case is different in "Why the Chisholm Trail Forks," which Stubb "tells scary" for the benefit of a tenderfoot nicknamed Lucy, who wants to know why the Chisholm Trail just north of the Cimarron sends out a new branch that goes its own way and then returns to the old trail seven miles above. The real explanation is that the alternate stretch gives better footing to the cattle; but Stubb feeds Lucy a long tale about a quarrel and a bloody gunfight between trail-driving outfits. Stubb lays it on thick, with plenty of tough dialogue. But he makes a slip which Lucy catches; Stubb weaves some actual graves into his story and Lucy notices that they are a long way from where Stubb's fictitious fight occurred. Lucy asks why the dead men were taken back to the sand hills for burial, but Stubb finds a ready answer —the sand was easier to dig. Anybody but a tenderfoot would have seen that the whole thing could never have happened. Stubb's story is the exaggerated, wild and woolly kind that Andy heartily disliked when presented seriously as true of the West. He carefully labeled "Why the Chisholm Trail Forks" as a tale for tenderfeet; it is hoped that no one will be taken in by it like poor Lucy.

There is no way of knowing how many of the tales in this collection Andy invented himself or had heard others tell. In his day he sat around many a campfire in Texas, the Indian Territory, and Kansas. He came to Texas in 1882 and worked on ranches and the trail for about ten years; then he spent a couple of years in Rockport, Texas, where he ran a grain and feed business with Joe Box; he was attracted by the mining boom in Cripple Creek and lived there for a short while until he became a resident of Colorado Springs in 1894.

Andy was born on May 3, 1859, in Whitley County, Indiana, where his parents owned a stock farm. At about the age of eighteen he ran away from home because in a family with no girls he frequently had to churn and wash dishes. While working at a lumber mill in Newport, Arkansas, he saw many shipments of Texas horses passing through to the north and decided to move on to Texas. An old-timer named H. C. Singer wrote J. Frank Dobie from Nixon on May 25, 1932, that he remembered seeing Andy Adams in San Antonio. "In 1882 he came to the Smith and Redmon Horse Yards and we all liked him as he was a plain nice boy. Geo. Redmon furnished him a horse and he went out with us to the pasture and eat and slept in the hayloft with us at night." Apparently Andy helped round up and drive horses into San Antonio. He made a trip to Live Oak County in 1882, and the next year he trailed a herd of horses to Caldwell, Kansas, where he happened to meet Frank Byler, a resident of Live Oak County and Mr. Dobie's maternal uncle. For several years he drove horses from Starr County on the Rio Grande to Peña, now Hebbronville, and shipped from there. While in the lower country he stayed off and on at El Sordo ranch between Peña and the settlement at the headquarters of old Rancho Randado; he kept some stock at El Sordo, but he was active in trading, rather than in raising, horses or cattle. El Sordo was owned by the Earnest brothers; Frank H. Earnest, nicknamed Red, and Andy became friends for life. Six miles away at Rancho Ibañez lived Tom Worsham, who became another of Andy's good friends. From Cotulla, seventy miles north of Laredo, Andy shipped horses across the Red River and drove them on to Kansas. Near the end of the trail days he turned to cattle and shipped out of Alice via the San Antonio and Aransas Pass Railway across Red River and then trailed them to the Cherokee Outlet. Adams and Box were too free with their credit in Rockport and they had to get out of the feed and seed business. Then Andy left for the gold field at Cripple Creek.

Joe Box, Frank Byler, and Red Earnest all appear in this collection of tales. Captain Redmon of Smith and Redmon Horse Yards does not, but he is mentioned in

A Texas Matchmaker (p. 222). In "Alkaline Dust Ain't Snow" Joe Box is hardly more than a name; he is one of the boys who hear Ace Gee's story in a saloon in Hennessey, Oklahoma, just before the Cherokee Strip is thrown open to settlement. In "Death of the Little Glassblower" he is one of the two big men that the dying man asks to stay by him until the end. The teller's brief description of Joe tallies with that given by Andy to J. Emerson Smith and quoted by him in the *Colorado Springs Gazette* (June 7, 1903, p. 11): "a tall, lanky, bald-headed fellow, the finest physical specimen of a man I've ever seen." In the course of telling "Strong on the Breed" Billy Honeyman says he had heard that "Byler had come in with a horse herd from the Nueces." Andy must have had in mind Frank Byler, who lived at Lagarto, just west of the Nueces, and who drove horses up the trail to Kansas. He and Andy happened to share a hotel room one time in Caldwell. "Captain" Frank Byler is Uncle Lance's guest on the horse hunt in the Nueces country during which Aaron Scales, Theodore Quayle, and Dan Happersett each tell a horse story.

Red Earnest is the teller and the principal person in "Cow Coroner for the Sap." Andy was reporting a true story, but it was Red's brother, Lee W. Earnest, who was claim agent for the Sap (the San Antonio and Aransas Pass Railway). Andy had Red tell one of Lee's experiences as his own at a campfire in Colorado. Mr. Pleasant Middagh, one of Andy's old camping companions, does not recall that Red ever came to Colorado to visit Andy. It is true, though, as Red says at the end of his tale, that he became a mounted inspector for the

U.S. Customs Service on the Rio Grande. Andy dedicated *A Texas Matchmaker* to Frank W. Earnest; when asked to identify this man, Andy told a very fine story about his old friend. The reporter introduced some inaccuracies (Red was only three years older than Andy and he did not fight in the Civil War), but here is the story as it appeared in the *Denver Republican* (June 15, 1904, p. 6).

"Red Earnest was one of the finest men who ever rode the old Western trail. Now mark that fact, for it is a sweeping statement; hundreds of bully good men traveled that trail and knew and loved it like the pages of a well read book. Red had served with distinction in the confederate army, and he was so proud of the South he barely talked about it. Occasionally it broke out, and when it did, flames flew. Many were the nights we had the same watch, and somehow we rather hit it off. Of course he was what I considered an old man, but years as numbered in cities didn't count with us in those days on the plains. Red was always, drunk or sober, beastly dignified and considerate. He had a slow drawl from a sweet low Southern voice. His politeness was illustrated once on the Rendado rancho [really Randado, a Texas ranch then famous for its horses, now in Jim Hogg County] where we had secured an old bottle of rare cognac—smuggled goods. When we broke the seal from the bottle and pulled the cork there were several strangers in the improvised bar of the rancho. One of these strangers wore a clerical garb, and Red at once walked over to this gent and offered the bottle. His hospitality was promptly declined; but all the rest of us took a drink, or two. When the bottle was empty and we were riding toward our camp, I took Red to task for offering liquor to one of the sacred cloth and asked him if he hadn't noticed his clothes. Red replied in his usual drawl, 'Well—son—I—thought—he—was—a—preacher—but—I didn't—propose—Sir—to slight—him—on that—account.' And to the memory of Earnest's proved, innate politeness, I dedicated the pages of the 'Texas Matchmaker.' "

Captain Kenedy of the Laurel Leaf ranch, one of the promoters of the Sap, is taken over directly from life into Red Earnest's story of the attempted swindle. Judge Roy Bean is himself in "Judge Bean in Court," whether the events of the tale took place or not. Theodore Baughman, whom Andy often calls Baugh for short, was a real person; Andy puts him in "The Marshal of Cow Springs" as a trail foreman. He is the principal actor in another story of Andy's, "Seigerman's Per Cent," which has been excluded from this collection because it does not qualify as a campfire tale. Charlie Siringo, Andy's friend from the time of the old Caldwell days, tells an anecdote about Baughman (disguised as Baufman) in *A Cowboy Detective* (Chicago: W. B. Conkey Company, 1912, p. 15): a blind phrenologist felt of Baughman's head bumps and said, "Ladies and gentlemen, here is a man who, if the Indians were on the warpath and he should run across one lone Indian on the plains, he would tell his friends that he had seen a thousand warriors." Baughman wrote a book about his adventures, *The Oklahoma Scout* (Chicago: Belford, Clarke & Co., 1886), which at no point measures up to the level of the campfire tale that Andy ascribes to him, "He Had Collided with Lead in Texas." This tale has to do with an unnamed man who holds up a stagecoach in Colorado and is captured the same day. At his trial he admits that a Texas court convicted him of robbing the mails in 1877 and sentenced him to ninety-nine years in military prison, from which he was released because he had influence with the President. Nor does he remain very long in prison after his second conviction. This robber can be identified as Ham White of Bastrop County, whose history was very much the same. (See J. S. Gallegly, "Background and Patterns of O. Henry's Texas Badman Stories," *Rice Institute Pamphlet*, XLII [1955], 10–12.)

Other real persons, whether under their own names or not, could no doubt be found in these campfire tales. One would suppose that a name like Quince Forrest was invented by Andy, but a student who had just read the *Log* assured me that his father had known a man by that name who used to be a trail driver. Nat Straw and Pete Slaughter, who are not mentioned in the campfire tales, are characters in the *Log;* their names sound invented too, but Nat Straw and Pete Slaughter were real enough, and Slaughter did direct the building of the brush-and-dirt bridge over the Big Boggy in Kansas—Andy got the details from Slaughter himself. Apparently Andy liked proper names taken from common nouns, such as Officer, Blades, Scales, Trotter, Pickett, and Quayle. It is dangerous to assume that names like these are fictitious. Waterwall sounds unreal, even farfetched; but there was a family of Waterwalls in Rockport, and George E. Waterwall used to buy feed for his dairy cows from Adams and Box. It is also dangerous to assume that a character with the name of a real person does and says in the tale what the person did and said in real life. From a literary point of view, the question of what is fictitious and what is real or historical is not all-important, no matter how interesting it may be. Andy had a respect for the truth of history and of everyday life, and he avoided the strained, improbable, and exaggerated. Yet he knew that imagination is an indispensable part of the writer's art. He used reality without doing violence to it or being unduly constrained by it. In a letter to Walter Prescott Webb (March 2, 1924), he says, "Fiction must be a reflex of life, hence the homely setting, the fire on the hearth, the cattle in the fields, after which, human imagination peoples it with men and women who are fictional, but are a mirrored reflection of those that we know in the flesh."

Andy's rendering of the language used by tellers of the campfire tales is in keeping with his general literary attitude. It is colorful and appropriate but not overdone or exaggerated. It is the language of cowboys and Rangers reworked and made smoother than it actually was. Though it has the ring of real talk, it could hardly be studied by a modern scholar as an altogether accurate and reliable specimen of the language of the Southwest in the seventies and eighties. Andy has done what most writers attempt to do when they have to represent a specialized or localized way of talking: he has retained the idioms and figures and improved the grammar and connection. The result that he obtains is convincing and lively. All of Andy's storytellers speak approximately the same language, with little individual variation. If the names of the tellers were scrambled, it would be very difficult to sort them out and attach them to the proper stories. The stories told by cowmen and those told by the Rangers could perhaps be distinguished by the less frequent occurrence of "cow talk" in the Ranger stories, leaving out of consideration the difference in subject matter. Andy's own language is less figurative and racy than that of his narrators; it has a quiet dignity that sometimes leans toward formality. Now and then he makes a grammatical slip; as he once said of himself, "The loop of his rope may settle on the wrong foot of the rhetoric occasionally."

Many of the sentences in the stories sound as lifelike as if Andy had written them down on the spot where he heard them. "There was a fellow drifted into the ranch where I was working, dead broke," says Wyatt Roundtree. At the beginning of his story about the making of the doughnuts, John Officer says, "The boys had blowed in their summer's wages and were feeling glum all over." When he reaches the point in the story where John Smith and four of his peelers ride in for some doughnuts, Officer says, "Company that way, you can't say anything." Priding himself on his drinking ability, Hugh Trotter says, "I can drink a week and never sleep; that's the kind of build to have if you expect to travel and meet all comers." Ace Gee says in the course of his story, "We had several bobbles crossing that strip of country; just jump and run a mile or so, and then mill until daylight."

There is an abundance of language drawn from the working of cattle and horses and applied to human beings and human situations. Once when Quince Forrest interrupts Officer's story, Officer tells Quince to "hobble his lip." Fox Quarternight comments on the preference that girls will sometimes show for a stranger: "To be sure, if she took a smile to this stranger, no other fellow could check her with a three-quarter rope and a snubbing post." While pretending to buy a hat for a dining-room girl in Fort Worth, one of the boys expresses his high opinion of her: "She can ride a string of my horses until they all have sore backs." To pay for the dozen blankets that he is buying for the boys after breaking the monte game, Big Tom empties his money on the counter and tells the storekeeper to "cut out" what he wants, as if the necessary dollars and bills were so many cattle to be separated from a herd.

Perhaps this is the place to comment on two words that are used in a very unfamiliar way. In his story Stubb says, "It would be a sin and shame to waste good liquor on paltry like them." Instead of *paltry* the original in *Cattle Brands* had *plafry,* which has no meaning at all. The context calls for a collective noun with a connotation of contempt. *Palfrey* is in Andy's vocabulary as a playful substitute for *horse,* but it is neither collective nor contemptuous. *Poultry* might possibly be the word intended, but a printer working from typed copy would hardly set *plafry* for it. On typographical grounds *paltry* is a more likely reading; as for sense, *paltry* occurs in some English dialects as a noun meaning "rubbish." There is another word that Andy seems to use in a highly dialectal or long-obsolete sense. Bull Durham says in his tale about the vigilantes, "The next morning I was given my breakfast; my horse, well cuffed and saddled, was brought to the door. . . ." All dictionaries failed me on the word *cuffed,* but M. P. Tilley's book of sixteenth- and seventeenth-century English proverbs turned up this: "Cuft catt's no good on mouse-hunt." In other versions of the proverb the words *muffled* and *muzzled* replace *cuffed.* It seems, then, that *cuffed* in Durham's sentence would mean nothing more than "bridled." In this sense *cuffed* was never a part of the Westerner's vocabulary. It might have been a very old survival preserved in Andy's Scotch-Irish family. Could *cuffed* in the story mean "curried" or "brushed"? One man whose whole business is horses has told me that he believes he has heard the word so used. It is not very likely, but *cuffed* might conceivably be a misprint for *curried.*

It has been stated above that Andy's own language differs from that of the tellers of the campfire tales. It would be very interesting to have a campfire tale that Andy told in his own person without any sort of pretended narrator, but unfortunately no such tale exists. *Reed Anthony, Cowman* (1907) has two potential campfire tales (pp. 157–59 and 374–75); they are not, however, live-voice tales and Reed Anthony's style is rather stiff. The story that Andy gave the reporter about Red Earnest, quoted above, might have been made into a campfire tale, though it would not have been typical of the tales in this collection. There is another story of Andy's that would have made a very fine campfire tale; it formed part of a lecture that he gave to the Men's League of the First Presbyterian Church in Colorado Springs on April 17, 1906. This lecture, called "The Cattle on a Thousand Hills," was published three years after Andy's death (1935), with some omissions, in the *Colorado Magazine* (XV [1938], 168–80). Andy included the story of the swimming ox in order to make a point.

"The use of an ox, as a saddle animal, recalls an incident which came under my observation. On the trail, one spring we lay for nearly a week waterbound with a freshet in Red River. During the delay of high water, herd after herd arrived, until there was within striking distance of the old ford fully fifty thousand cattle and over two hundred men. Every day, not less than one hundred well-mounted horsemen gathered at the crossing, noting the condition of the river and to exchange the chronicles of the day. Everyone was impatient to cross, as the cattle were congesting on the Texas side, the close proximity of the herds making the risk dangerous in case of a stampede by night. Instead of the freshet falling, it gradually rose, overflowing the banks and lower bottoms, while driftwood and other debris was borne downstream with the onrushing flood, the waters being fully three hundred yards wide. Frequently, large trees floated by, swirling and turning as the angry currents toyed with the flotsam of the flood, while the muddy river itself rolled on, disputing our advance.

"Across the stream stood a general store, and, like forbidden fruit to children, every man amongst us wanted to cross and price its wares. Scarcely a day passed but some daring lad would attempt to swim the river on his horse, and in every case was forced to return to the Texas side. Frequently, half a dozen would make the effort together, first awaiting an opportunity until the channel was fairly free of driftwood; but the eddying currents caught men and horses and ducked them like toys, both swimming for their lives to regain the nearest friendly shore, and often landing fully a mile below the entrance of the ford.

"Matters ran along this way for five or six days, none of which were allowed to pass without some daring spirit making the attempt to reach that store, so near and yet so far, when one evening a freighter drove up. His team consisted of ten yoke of oxen, drawing a lead and two trail wagons, behind the rear one of which was led a good saddle horse. On the arrival of this wayfarer of the plains, there were an unusual number of men present from the different herds, and speculation ran high as to what this freighter would do. He camped within sight of the crossing, quietly unyoking his team, belling several of them, and finally tied a large black wheel ox to the wagon. After picketing his horse and making things snug for the night, he led his big wheeler down to the ford, hastily made a halter out of the rope and, without inquiry of the hundred or more men present, mounted his ox bareback and put into the river. We admired his nerve, though we doubted his discretion, and I feel positive that every rascal amongst us, who had met defeat in those waters, secretly wished them to rebuff the freighter. But, guided by the word of his master, that big black ox swam like a swan, picked his way through the driftwood, breasted and quartered the swift currents, and finally, to our unanimous disgust, landed safe and sound on the farther bank.

"The teamster lazily dismounted, turned the ox loose to graze, went up to the store and almost immediately returned, leading his mount well upstream before reentering the river. On the return trip they encountered some dangerous driftwood, but the voice of the master reached us, cautiously talking to his ox and, when the crisis safely passed, shamed by our envy, we shouted encouragement. The teamster waved his hand in reply, landing shortly afterward, squarely in the entrance to the ford, and we greeted him as a victor. Curiosity, however, ran high as to his errand across the river at such a risk and, as there was no visible reason, our inquisitiveness was aroused. Men whispered to one another and, as the freighter led his ox up the bank and turned him loose, a foreman of one of the herds detained him long enough to ask, 'Say, pardner, what in the name of common sense did you swim that river for, anyhow?'

" 'Why, I was out of tobacco,' innocently replied the teamster. 'Any of you boys care to smoke?'

"The point I wish to make from this incident is this: In physical courage that freighter had no advantage over those trail men, as the latter were known for their daring, and all credit must be given the ox. With the seventeen herds that lay waterbound on this occasion, there were fully two thousand picked horses, and no lack of riders to dare the flood, but it remained for an ox to force the passage, and doing it as easily as one might walk from church to home. The ox, and not the rider, deserved the credit of the feat."

What a wonderful campfire tale this would have made! It is strange that Andy did not have Billy Honeyman, Joe Stallings, or one of the other boys tell it. As good as it is in its present form, it would have been even better in free and racy cowboy talk, told to the most fitting listeners in the world, other cowboys with their backs against a wheel of the chuck wagon or their heads propped up on a saddle, gazing into the fire. Waterbound at Red River, with every oncoming herd adding to the danger of a stampede and a general mix-up—this is the situation described at the beginning of "Cow Coroner for the Sap." When the river began to fall, Red Earnest was elected foreman of all the outfits and saw that sixty-five thousand cattle were swum across the river without a mishap.

Set apart from the novels and longer stories in which they occur and brought together in one book, Andy's campfire tales should have no trouble in making their own way in the literary world.

Andy Adams' Campfire Tales

Bull Durham and the Vigilantes

told by
Bull Durham

It proved an ideal camp, with wood, water, and grass in abundance, and very little range stock to annoy us. We had watered the herd just before noon, and before throwing them upon the bed-ground for the night, watered them a second time. We had a splendid campfire that night, of dry live-oak logs, and after supper was over and the first guard had taken the herd, smoking and storytelling were the order of the evening. The campfire is to all outdoor life what the evening fireside is to domestic life. After the labors of the day are over, the men gather around the fire, and the social hour of the day is spent in yarning. The stories told may run from the sublime to the ridiculous, from a true incident to a base fabrication, or from a touching bit of pathos to the most vulgar vulgarity.

"Have I ever told this outfit my experience with the vigilantes when I was a kid?" inquired Bull Durham. There was a general negative response, and he proceeded. "Well, our folks were living on the Frio at the time, and there was a man in our neighborhood who had an outfit of four men out beyond Nueces canyon hunting wild cattle for their hides. It was necessary to take them out supplies about every so often, and on one trip he begged my folks to let me go along for company. I was a slim slip of a colt about fourteen at the time, and as this man was a friend of ours, my folks consented to let me go along. We each had a good saddle horse, and two pack mules with provisions and ammunition for the hunting camp. The first night we made camp, a boy overtook us with the news that the brother of my companion had been accidentally killed by a horse, and of course he would have to return. Well, we were twenty miles on our way, and as it would take some little time to go back and return with the loaded mules, I volunteered, like a fool kid, to go on and take the packs through.

"The only question was, could I pack and unpack. I had helped him at this work, double-handed, but now that I was to try it alone, he showed me what he called a squaw hitch, with which you can lash a pack single-handed. After putting me through it once or twice, and satisfying himself that I could do the packing, he consented to let me go on, he and the messenger returning home during the night. The next morning I packed without any trouble and started on my way. It would take me two days yet, poking along with heavy packs, to reach the hunters. Well, I hadn't made over eight or ten miles the first morning, when, as I rounded a turn in the trail, a man stepped out from behind a rock, threw a gun in my face, and ordered me to hold up my hands. Then another appeared from the opposite side with his gun leveled on me. Inside of half a minute a dozen men galloped up from every quarter, all armed to the teeth. The man on leaving had given me his gun for company, one of these old smoke-pole, cap-and-ball six-shooters, but I must have forgotten what guns were for, for I elevated my little hands nicely. The leader of the party questioned me as to who I was, and what I was doing there, and what I had in those packs. That once, at least, I told the truth. Every mother's son of them was cursing and cross-questioning me in the same breath. They ordered me off my horse, took my gun, and proceeded to verify my tale by unpacking the mules. So much ammunition aroused their suspicions, but my story was as good as it was true, and they never shook me from the truth of it. I soon learned that robbery was not their motive, and the leader explained the situation.

"A vigilance committee had been in force in that county for some time, trying to rid the country of lawless characters. But lawlessness got into the saddle, and had bench warrants issued and served on every member of this vigilance committee. As the vigilantes numbered several hundred, there was no jail large enough to hold such a number, so they were released on parole for appearance at court. When court met, every man served with a capias—"

"Hold on! hold your horses just a minute," interrupted Quince Forrest. "I want to get that word. I want to make a memorandum of it, for I may want to use it myself sometime. Capias? Now I have it; go ahead."

"When court met, every man served with a bench warrant from the judge presiding was present, and as soon as court was called to order, a squad of men arose in the courtroom, and the next moment the judge fell riddled with lead. Then the factions scattered to fight it out, and I was passing through the county while matters were active.

"They confiscated my gun and all the ammunition in the packs, but helped me to repack and started me on my way. A happy thought struck one of the men to give me a letter, which would carry me through without further trouble, but the leader stopped him, saying, 'Let the boy alone. Your letter would hang him as sure as hell's hot, before he went ten miles farther.' I declined the letter. Even then I didn't have sense enough to turn back, and inside of two hours I was rounded up by the other faction. I had learned my story perfectly by this time, but those packs had to come off again for everything to be examined. There was nothing in them now but flour and salt and such things—nothing that they might consider suspicious. One fellow in this second party took a fancy to my horse, and offered to help hang me on general principles, but kinder counsels prevailed. They also helped me to repack, and I started on once more. Before I reached my destination the following evening, I was held up seven different times. I got so used to it that I was happily disappointed every shelter I passed, if some man did not step out and throw a gun in my face.

"I had trouble to convince the cattle hunters of my experiences, but the absence of any ammunition, which they needed worst, at last led them to give credit to my tale. I was expected home within a week, as I was to go down on the Nueces on a cow hunt which was making up, and I only rested one day at the hunters' camp. On their advice, I took a different route on my way home, leaving the mules behind me. I never saw a man the next day returning, and was feeling quite gala on my good fortune. When evening came on, I sighted a little ranch house some distance off the trail, and concluded to ride to it and stay overnight. As I approached, I saw that some one lived there, as there were chickens and dogs about, but not a person in sight. I dismounted and knocked on the door, when, without a word, the door was thrown wide open and a half-dozen guns were poked into my face. I was ordered into the house and given a chance to tell my story again. Whether my story was true or not, they took no chances on me, but kept me all night. One of the men took my horse to the stable and cared for him, and I was well fed and given a place to sleep, but not a man offered a word of explanation, from which I took it they did not belong to the vigilance faction. When it came time to go to bed, one man said to me, 'Now, sonny, don't make any attempt to get away, and don't move out of your bed without warning us, for you'll be shot as sure as you do. We won't harm a hair on your head if you're telling us the truth; only do as you're told, for we'll watch you.'

"By this time I had learned to obey orders while in that county, and got a fair night's sleep, though there were men going and coming all night. The next morning I was given my breakfast; my horse, well cuffed and saddled, was brought to the door, and with this parting advice I was given permission to go: 'Son, if you've told us the truth, don't look back when you ride away. You'll be watched for the first ten miles after leaving here, and if you've lied to us it will go hard with you. Now, remember, don't look back, for these are times when no one cares to be identified.' I never questioned that man's advice; it was 'die dog or eat the hatchet' with me. I mounted my horse, waved the usual parting courtesies, and rode away. As I turned into the trail about a quarter mile from the house, I noticed two men ride out from behind the stable and follow me. I remembered the story about Lot's wife looking back, though it was lead and not miracles that I was afraid of that morning.

"For the first hour I could hear the men talking and the hoofbeats of their horses, as they rode along always the same distance behind me. After about two hours of this one-sided joke, as I rode over a little hill, I looked out of the corner of my eye back at my escort, still about a quarter of a mile behind me. One of them noticed me and raised his gun, but I instantly changed my view, and the moment the hill hid me, put spurs to my horse, so that when they reached the brow of the hill, I was half a mile in the lead, burning the earth like a canned dog. They threw lead close around me, but my horse lengthened the distance between us for the next five miles, when they dropped entirely out of sight. By noon I came into the old stage road, and by the middle of the afternoon reached home after over sixty miles in the saddle without a halt."

Just at the conclusion of Bull's story, Flood rode in from the herd, and after picketing his horse, joined the circle. For fully an hour after the return of our foreman, we lounged around the fire, during which there was a full and free discussion of stampedes. But finally, Flood, suiting the action to the word by arising, suggested that all hands hunt their blankets and turn in for the night. A quiet wink from Bull to several of the boys held us for the time being, and innocently turning to Forrest, Durham inquired,

"Where was—when was—was it you that was telling someone about a run you were in last summer? I never heard you tell it. Where was it?"

"You mean on the Cimarron last year when we mixed two herds," said Quince, who had taken the bait like a bass and was now fully embarked on a yarn. "We were in rather close quarters, herds ahead and behind us, when one night here came a cow herd like a cyclone and swept right through our camp. We tumbled out of our blankets and ran for our horses, but before we could bridle—"

Bull had given us the wink, and every man in the outfit fell back, and the snoring that checked the storyteller was like a chorus of ripsaws running through pine knots. Forrest took in the situation at a glance, and as he arose to leave, looked back and remarked—

"You must all think that's smart."

Before he was out of hearing, Durham said to the rest of us—

"A few doses like that will cure him of sucking eggs and acting smart, interrupting folks."

The Quarternights near the Salt Licks

told by
***Fox** Quarternight*

At our last camp at the lakes, the Rebel and I, as partners, had been shamefully beaten in a game of seven-up by Bull Durham and John Officer, and had demanded satisfaction in another trial around the fire that night. We borrowed McCann's lantern, and by the aid of it and the campfire had an abundance of light for our game. In the absence of a table, we unrolled a bed and sat down Indian fashion over a game of cards in which all friendship ceased.

The outfit, with the exception of myself, had come from the same neighborhood, and an item in Honeyman's letter causing considerable comment was a wedding which had occurred since the outfit had left. It seemed that a number of the boys had sparked the bride in times past, and now that she was married, their minds naturally became reminiscent over old sweethearts.

"The way I make it out," said Honeyman, in commenting on the news, "is that the girl had met this fellow over in the next county while visiting her cousins the year before. My sister gives it as a horseback opinion that she'd been engaged to this fellow nearly eight months; girls, you know, sabe each other that way. Well, it won't affect my appetite any if all the girls I know get married while I'm gone."

"You certainly have never experienced the tender passion," said Fox Quarternight to our horse wrangler, as he lighted his pipe with a brand from the fire. "Now I have. That's the reason why I sympathize with these old beaus of the bride. Of course, I was too old to stand any show on her string, and I reckon the fellow who got her ain't so powerful much, except his veneering and being a stranger, which was a big advantage. To be sure, if she took a smile to this stranger, no other fellow could check her with a three-quarter rope and a snubbing post. I've seen girls walk right by a dozen good fellows and fawn over some scrub. My experience teaches me that when there's a woman in it, it's haphazard potluck with no telling which way the cat will hop. You can't play any system, and merit cuts little figure in general results."

"Fox," said Durham, while Officer was shuffling the cards, "your auger seems well oiled and working keen tonight. Suppose you give us that little experience of yours in love affairs. It will be a treat to those of us who have never been in love, and won't interrupt the game a particle. Cut loose, won't you?"

"It's a long time back," said Quarternight, meditatively, "and the scars have all healed, so I don't mind telling it. I was born and raised on the border of the Blue Grass Region in Kentucky. I had the misfortune to be born of poor but honest parents, as they do in stories; no hero ever had the advantage of me in that respect. In love affairs, however, it's a high card in your hand to be born rich. The country around my old home had good schools, so we had the advantage of a good education. When I was about nineteen, I went away from home one winter to teach school—a little country school about fifteen miles from home. But in the old states fifteen miles from home makes you a dead rank stranger. The trustee of the township was shucking corn when I went to apply for the school. I simply whipped out my peg and helped him shuck out a shock or two while we talked over school matters. The dinner bell rang, and he insisted on my staying for dinner with him. Well, he gave me a better school than I had asked for—better neighborhood, he said—and told me to board with a certain family who had no children; he gave his reasons, but that's immaterial. They were friends of his, so I learned afterwards.

They proved to be fine people. The woman was one of those kindly souls who never know where to stop. She planned and schemed to marry me off in spite of myself. The first month that I was with them she told me all about the girls in that immediate neighborhood. In fact, she rather got me unduly excited, being a youth and somewhat verdant. She dwelt powerful heavy on a girl who lived in a big brick house which stood back of the road some distance. This girl had gone to school at a seminary for young ladies near Lexington—studied music and painting and was 'way up on everything. She described her to me as black-eyed with raven tresses, just like you read about in novels.

"Things were rocking along nicely, when a few days before Christmas a little girl who belonged to the family who lived in the brick house brought me a note one morning. It was an invitation to take supper with them the following evening. The note was written in a pretty hand, and the name signed to it—I'm satisfied now it was a forgery. My landlady agreed with me on that point; in fact, she may have mentioned it first. I never ought to have taken her into my confidence like I did. But I wanted to consult her, showed her the invitation, and asked her advice. She was in the seventh heaven of delight; had me answer it at once, accept the invitation with pleasure and a lot of stuff that I never used before —she had been young once herself. I used up five or six sheets of paper in writing the answer, spoilt one after another, and the one I did send was a flat failure compared to the one I received. Well, the next evening when it was time to start, I was nervous and uneasy. It was nearly dark when I reached the house, but I wanted it that way. Say, but when I knocked on the front door of that house it was with fear and trembling.

" 'Is this Mr. Quarternight?' inquired a very affable lady who received me.

"I knew I was one of old man Quarternight's seven boys, and admitted that that was my name, though it was the first time anyone had ever called me *mister*. I was welcomed, ushered in, and introduced all around. There were a few small children whom I knew, so I managed to talk to them. The girl whom I was being braced against was not a particle overrated, but sustained the Kentucky reputation for beauty. She made herself so pleasant and agreeable that my fears soon subsided. When the man of the house came in I was cured entirely. He was gruff and hearty, opened his mouth and laughed deep. I built right up to him. We talked about cattle and horses until supper was announced. He was really sorry I hadn't come earlier, so as to look at a three-year-old colt that he set a heap of store by. He showed him to me after supper with a lantern. Fine colt, too. I don't remember much about the supper, except that it was fine and I came near spilling my coffee several times, my hands were so large and my coat sleeves so short. When we returned from looking at the colt, we went into the parlor. Say, fellows, it was a little the nicest thing that ever I went against. Carpet that made you think you were going to bog down every step, springy like marsh land, and I was glad I came. Then the younger children were ordered to retire, and shortly afterward the man and his wife followed suit.

"When I heard the old man throw his heavy boots on the floor in the next room, I realized that I was left all alone with their charming daughter. All my fears of the early part of the evening tried to crowd on me again, but were calmed by the girl, who sang and played on the piano with no audience but me. Then she interested me by telling her school experiences, and how glad she was that they were over. Finally she lugged out a great big family album, and sat down aside of me on one of the horsehair sofas. That album had a clasp on it, a buckle of pure silver, same as these eighteen-dollar bridles. While we were looking at the pictures—some of the old varmints had fought in the Revolutionary War, so she said—I noticed how close we were sitting together. Then we sat farther apart after we had gone through the album, one on each end of the sofa, and talked about the neighborhood, until I suddenly remembered that I had to go. While she was getting my hat and I was getting away, somehow she had me promise to take dinner with them on Christmas.

"For the next two or three months it was hard to tell if I lived at my boarding house or at the brick. If I failed to go, my landlady would hatch up some errand and send me over. If she hadn't been such a good woman, I'd never forgive her for leading me to the sacrifice like she did. Well, about two weeks before school was out, I went home over Saturday and Sunday. Those were fatal days in my life. When I returned on Monday morning, there was a letter waiting for me. It was from the girl's mamma. There had been a quilting in the neighborhood on Saturday, and at this meet of the local gossips, someone had hinted that there was liable to be a wedding as soon as school was out. Mamma was present, and neither admitted nor denied the charge. But there was a woman at this quilting who had once lived over in our neighborhood and felt it her duty to enlighten the company as to who I was. I got all this later from my landlady.

" 'Law me,' said this woman, 'folks round here in this section think our teacher is the son of that big farmer who raises so many cattle and horses. Why, I've known both families of those Quarternights for nigh on to thirty year. Our teacher is one of old John Fox's boys, the Irish Quarternights, who live up near the salt licks on Doe Run. They were always so poor that the children never had enough to eat and hardly half enough to wear.'

"This plain statement of facts fell like a bombshell on mamma. She started a private investigation of her own, and her verdict was in that letter. It was a center shot. That evening when I locked the schoolhouse door it was for the last time, for I never unlocked it again. My landlady, dear old womanly soul, tried hard to have me teach the school out at least, but I didn't see it that way. The cause of education in Kentucky might have gone straight to eternal hell before I'd have stayed another day in that neighborhood. I had money enough to get to Texas with, and here I am. When a fellow gets it burnt into him like a brand that way once, it lasts him quite a while. He'll feel his way next time."

"That was rather a raw deal to give a fellow," said Officer, who had been listening while playing cards. "Didn't you never see the girl again?"

"No, nor you wouldn't want to either if that letter had been written to you. And some folks claim that seven is a lucky number; there were seven boys in our family and nary one ever married."

Strong on the Breed

told by
Billy Honeyman

That experience of Fox's," remarked Honeyman, after a short silence, "is almost similar to one I had. Before Lovell and Flood adopted me, I worked for a horse man down on the Nueces. Every year he drove up the trail a large herd of horse stock. We drove to the same point on the trail each year, and I happened to get acquainted up there with a family that had several girls in it. The youngest girl in the family and I seemed to understand each other fairly well. I had to stay at the horse camp most of the time, and in one way and another did not get to see her as much as I would have liked. When we sold out the herd, I hung around for a week or so, and spent a month's wages showing her the cloud with the silver lining. She stood it all easy, too. When the outfit went home, of course I went with them. I was banking plenty strong, however, that next year, if there was a good market in horses, I'd take her home with me. I had saved my wages and rustled around, and when we started up the trail next year, I had forty horses of my own in the herd. I had figured they would bring me a thousand dollars, and there was my wages besides.

"When we reached this place, we held the herd out twenty miles, so it was some time before I got into town to see the girl. But the first time I did get to see her I learned that an older sister of hers, who had run away with some renegade from Texas a year or so before, had drifted back home lately with tears in her eyes and a big fat baby boy in her arms. She warned me to keep away from the house, for men from Texas were at a slight discount right then in that family. The girl seemed to regret it and talked reasonable, and I thought I could see encouragement. I didn't crowd matters, nor did her folks forget me when they heard that Byler had come in with a horse herd from the Nueces. I met the girl away from home several times during the summer, and learned that they kept hot water on tap to scald me if I ever dared to show up. One son-in-law from Texas had simply surfeited that family—there was no other vacancy.

"About the time we closed out and were again ready to go home, there was a cattleman's ball given in this little trail town. We stayed over several days to take in this ball, as I had some plans of my own. My girl was at the ball all easy enough, but she warned me that her brother was watching me. I paid no attention to him, and danced with her right along, begging her to run away with me. It was obviously the only play to make. But the more I'd 'suade her the more she'd 'fuse. The family was on the prod bigger than a wolf, and there was no use reasoning with them. After I had had every dance with her for an hour or so, her brother coolly stepped in and took her home. The next morning he felt it his duty, as his sister's protector, to hunt me up and inform me that if I even spoke to his sister again, he'd shoot me like a dog.

" 'Is that a bluff, or do you mean it for a real play?' I inquired, politely.

" 'You'll find that it will be real enough,' he answered angrily.

" 'Well, now, that's too bad,' I answered; 'I'm really sorry that I can't promise to respect your request. But this much I can assure you: any time that you have the leisure and want to shoot me, just cut loose your dog. But remember this one thing—that it will be my second shot.'

"I hung up my gentle honk before his eyes and ears and gave him free license to call it. The truth is, I didn't pay any more attention to him than I would to an empty bottle. I reckon the girl was all right, but the family were these razor-backed, barnyard savages. It makes me hot under the collar yet when I think of it. They'd have lawed me if I had, but I ought to have shot him and checked the breed."

"Why didn't you run off with her?" inquired Fox, dryly.

"Well, of course a man of your nerve is always capable of advising others. But you see, I'm strong on the breed. Now a girl can't show her true colors like the girl's brother did, but get her in the harness once, and then she'll show you the white of her eye, balk, and possibly kick over the wagon tongue. No, I believe in the breed—blood'll tell."

The Genuine Blend of Bluegrass and Bourbon

told by
Wyatt Roundtree

Though it was a lovely summer night, we had a fire, and supper over, the conversation ranged wide and free. As the wagon on the trail is home, naturally the fire is the hearthstone, so we gathered and lounged around it.

"The only way to enjoy such a fine night as this," remarked Ash, "is to sit up smoking until you fall asleep with your boots on. Between too much sleep and just enough, there's a happy medium which suits me."

"Officer," inquired Wyatt Roundtree, trailing into the conversation very innocently, "why is it that people who live up among those Yankees always say 'be' the remainder of their lives?"

"What's the matter with the word?" countered Officer.

"Oh, nothing, I reckon, only it sounds a little odd, and there's a tale to it."

"A story, you mean," said Officer, reprovingly.

"Well, I'll tell it to you," said Roundtree, "and then you can call it to suit yourself. It was out in New Mexico where this happened. There was a fellow drifted into the ranch where I was working, dead broke. To make matters worse, he could do nothing; he wouldn't fit anywhere. Still, he was a nice fellow and we all liked him. Must have had a good education, for he had good letters from people up North. He had worked in stores and had once clerked in a bank, at least the letters said so. Well, we put up a job to get him a place in a little town out on the railroad. You all know how clannish Kentuckians are. Let two meet who never saw each other before, and inside of half an hour they'll be chewing tobacco from the same plug and trying to loan each other money."

"That's just like them," interposed Fox Quarternight.

"Well, there was an old man lived in this town, who was the genuine blend of bluegrass and bourbon. If another Kentuckian came within twenty miles of him, and he found it out, he'd hunt him up and they'd hold a two-handed reunion. We put up the job that this young man should play that he was a Kentuckian, hoping that the old man would take him to his bosom and give him something to do. So we took him into town one day, coached and fully posted how to act and play his part. We met the old man in front of his place of business, and, after the usual comment on the news over our way, weather, and other small talk, we were on the point of passing on, when one of our own crowd turned back and inquired, 'Uncle Henry, have you met the young Kentuckian who's in the country?'

" 'No,' said the old man, brightening with interest, 'who is he and where is he?'

" 'He's in town somewhere,' volunteered one of the boys. We pretended to survey the street from where we stood, when one of the boys blurted out, 'Yonder he stands now. That fellow in front of the drugstore over there, with the hard-boiled hat on.'

"The old man started for him, angling across the street, in disregard of sidewalks. We watched the meeting, thinking it was working all right. We were mistaken. We saw them shake hands, when the old man turned and walked away very haughtily. Something had gone wrong. He took the sidewalk on his return, and when he came near enough to us, we could see that he was angry and on the prod. When he came near enough to speak, he said, 'You think you're smart, don't you? He's a Kentuckian, is he? Hell's full of such Kentuckians!' And as he passed beyond hearing he was muttering imprecations on us. The young fellow joined us a minute later with the question, 'What kind of a crank is that you ran me up against?'

" 'He's as nice a man as there is in this country,' said one of the crowd. 'What did you say to him?'

" 'Nothing; he came up to me, extended his hand, saying, "My young friend, I understand that you're from Kentucky." "I be, sir," I replied, when he looked me in the eye and said, "You're a G—— d—— liar," and turned and walked away. Why, he must have wanted to insult me.'

"And then we all knew why our little scheme had failed. There was food and raiment in it for him, but he would use that little word 'be'."

Joe Jenks' Pet Ox

told by
Quince Forrest

Quince Forrest, who had brought in his horse to go out with the second watch, he and Bob Blades having taken advantage of the foreman's absence to change places on guard for the night, had been listening to the latter part of Wyatt's yarn very attentively. We all hoped that he would mount and ride out to the herd, for though he was a good storyteller and meaty with personal experiences, where he thought they would pass muster he was inclined to overcolor his statements. We usually gave him respectful attention, but were frequently compelled to regard him as a cheerful, harmless liar. So when he showed no disposition to go, we knew we were in for one from him.

"When I was boss bull-whacker," he began, "for a big army sutler at Fort Concho, I used to make two round trips a month with my train. It was a hundred miles to wagon from the freight point where we got our supplies. I had ten teams, six and seven yoke to the team, and trail wagons to each. I was furnished a night herder and a cook, saddle horses for both night herder and myself. You hear me, it was a slam-up fine layout. We could handle three or four tons to the team, and with the whole train we could chamber two carloads of anything. One day we were nearing the fort with a mixed cargo of freight, when a messenger came out and met us with an order from the sutler. He wanted us to make the fort that night and unload. The mail buckboard had reported us to the sutler as camped out back on a little creek about ten miles. We were always entitled to a day to unload and drive back to camp, which gave us good grass for the oxen, but under the orders the whips popped merrily that afternoon, and when they all got well strung out, I rode in ahead, to see what was up. Well, it seems that four companies of infantry from Fort McKavett, which were out for field practice, were going to be brought into this post to be paid three months' wages. This, with the troops stationed at Concho, would turn loose quite a wad of money. The sutler called me into his office when I reached the fort, and when he had produced a black bottle used for cutting the alkali in your drinking water, he said, 'Jack'—he called me Jack; my full name is John Quincy Forrest—'Jack, can you make the round trip, and bring in two cars of bottled beer that will be on the track waiting for you, and get back by pay day, the 10th?'

"I figured the time in my mind; it was twelve days.

" 'There's five extra in it for each man for the trip, and I'll make it right with you,' he added, as he noticed my hesitation, though I was only making a mental calculation.

" 'Why, certainly, Captain,' I said. 'What's that fable about the jack rabbit and the land terrapin?' He didn't know and I didn't either, so I said to illustrate the point: 'Put your freight on a bull train, and it always goes through on time. A race horse can't beat an ox on a hundred miles and repeat to a freight wagon.' Well, we unloaded before night, and it was pitch dark before we made camp. I explained the situation to the men. We planned to go in empty in five days, which would give us seven to come back loaded. We made every camp on time like clockwork. The fifth morning we were anxious to get a daybreak start, so we could load at night. The night herder had his orders to bring in the oxen the first sign of day, and I called the cook an hour before light. When the oxen were brought in, the men were up and ready to go to yoking. But the nigh wheeler in Joe Jenks' team, a big brindle muley ox, a regular pet steer, was missing. I saw him myself, Joe saw him, and the night herder swore he came in with the rest. Well, we looked high and low for that Mr. Ox, but he had vanished. While the men were eating their breakfast, I got on my horse and the night herder and I scoured and circled that country for miles around, but no ox. The country was so bare and level that a jack rabbit needed to carry a fly for shade. I was worried, for we needed every ox and every moment of time. I ordered Joe to tie his mate behind the trail wagon and pull out one ox shy.

"Well, fellows, that thing worried me powerful. Half the teamsters, good, honest, truthful men as ever popped a whip, swore they saw that ox when they came in. Well, it served a strong argument that a man can be positive and yet be mistaken. We nooned ten miles from our night camp that day. Jerry Wilkens happened to mention it at dinner that he believed his trail needed greasing. 'Why,' said Jerry, 'you'd think that I was loaded, the way my team kept their chains taut.' I noticed Joe get up from dinner before he had finished, as if an idea had struck him. He went over and opened the sheet in Jerry's trail wagon, and a smile spread over his countenance. 'Come here, fellows,' was all he said.

"We ran over to the wagon and there—"

The boys turned their backs with indistinct mutterings of disgust.

"You all don't need to believe this if you don't want to, but there was the missing ox, coiled up and sleeping like a bear in the wagon. He even had Jerry's roll of bedding for a pillow. You see, the wagon sheet was open in front, and he had hopped up on the trail tongue and crept in there to steal a ride. Joe climbed into the wagon, and gave him a few swift kicks in the short ribs, when he opened his eyes, yawned, got up, and jumped out."

Bull was rolling a cigarette before starting, while Fox's night horse was hard to bridle, which hindered them. With this slight delay, Forrest turned his horse back and continued, "That same ox on the next trip, one night when we had the wagons parked into a corral, got away from the herder, tiptoed over the men's beds in the gate, stood on his hind legs long enough to eat four fifty-pound sacks of flour out of the rear end of a wagon, got down on his side, and wormed his way under the wagon back into the herd, without being detected or waking a man."

As they rode away to relieve the first guard, McCann said, "Isn't he a muzzle-loading daisy? If I loved a liar I'd hug that man to death."

There's My Horse's Track

told by
Billy Honeyman

As soon as supper was over and the first guard had taken the herd, the poker game opened, each man being given ten beans for chips. We were playing for the wild turkey egg that would be left over after the sixteen that I had found in the morning were divided among us. We had only one deck of cards, so one game was all that could be run at a time, but there were six players, and when one was frozen out another sat in and took his place. As wood was plentiful, we had a good fire, and this with the aid of the cook's lantern gave an abundance of light. We unrolled a bed to serve as a table, sat down on it Indian fashion, and as fast as one seat was vacated there was a man ready to fill it, for we were impatient for our turns in the game. The talk turned on an accident which had happened that afternoon. While we were crossing the North Fork of the Canadian, Bob Blades attempted to ride out of the river below the crossing, when his horse bogged down. He instantly dismounted, and his horse after floundering around scrambled out and up the bank, but with a broken leg. Our foreman had ridden up and ordered the horse unsaddled and shot, to put him out of his suffering.

While waiting our turns, the accident to the horse was referred to several times, and finally Blades, who was sitting in the game, turned to us who were lounging around the fire, and asked, "Did you all notice that look he gave me as I was uncinching the saddle? If he had been human, he might have told what that look meant. Good thing he was a horse and couldn't realize."

From then on, the yarning and conversation was strictly *horse.*

"It was always a mystery to me," said Billy Honeyman, "how a Mexican or Indian knows so much more about a horse than any of us. I have seen them trail a horse across a country for miles, riding in a long lope, with not a trace or sign visible to me. I was helping a horseman once to drive a herd of horses to San Antonio from the lower Rio Grande country. We were driving them to market, and as there were no railroads south then, we had to take along saddle horses to ride home on after disposing of the herd. We always took favorite horses which we didn't wish to sell, generally two apiece for that purpose. This time, when we were at least a hundred miles from the ranch, a Mexican, who had brought along a pet horse to ride home, thought he wouldn't hobble this pet one night, fancying the animal wouldn't leave the others. Well, next morning his pet was missing. We scoured the country around and the trail we had come over for ten miles, but no horse. As the country was all open, we felt positive he would go back to the ranch.

"Two days later and about forty miles higher up the road, the Mexican was riding in the lead of the herd, when suddenly he reined in his horse, throwing him back on his haunches, and waved for some of us to come to him, never taking his eyes off what he saw in the road. The owner was riding on one point of the herd and I on the other. We hurried around to him and both rode up at the same time, when the vaquero blurted out, 'There's my horse's track.'

" 'What horse?' asked the owner.

" 'My own; the horse we lost two days ago,' replied the Mexican.

" 'How do you know it's your horse's track from the thousands of others that fill the road?' demanded his employer.

" 'Don Tomás,' said the Aztec, lifting his hat, 'how do I know your step or voice from a thousand others?'

"We laughed at him. He had been a peon, and that

made him respect our opinions—at least he avoided differing with us. But as we drove on that afternoon, we could see him in the lead, watching for that horse's track. Several times he turned in his saddle and looked back, pointed to some track in the road, and lifted his hat to us. At camp that night we tried to draw him out, but he was silent.

"But when we were nearing San Antonio, we overtook a number of wagons loaded with wool, lying over, as it was Sunday, and there among their horses and mules was our Mexican's missing horse. The owner of the wagons explained how he came to have the horse. The animal had come to his camp one morning, back about twenty miles from where we had lost him, while he was feeding grain to his work stock, and being a pet insisted on being fed. Since then, I have always had a lot of respect for a greaser's opinion regarding a horse."

"Turkey eggs is too rich for my blood," said Bob Blades, rising from the game. "I don't care a continental who wins the egg now, for whenever I get three queens pat beat by a four-card draw, I have misgivings about the deal. And old Quince thinks he can stack cards. He couldn't stack hay."

A Horse Herd Lost to Cheyennes

told by
Wyatt Roundtree

"Speaking about Mexicans and Indians," said Wyatt Roundtree, "I've got more use for a good horse than I have for either of those grades of humanity. I had a little experience over east here, on the cutoff from the Chisholm Trail, a few years ago, that gave me all the Injun I want for some time to come. A band of renegade Cheyennes had hung along the trail for several years, scaring or begging passing herds into giving them a beef. Of course, all the cattle herds had more or less strays among them, so it was easier to cut out one of these than to argue the matter. There was plenty of herds on the trail then, so this band of Indians got bolder than bandits. In the year I'm speaking of, I went up with a herd of horses belonging to a Texas man, who was in charge with us. When we came along with our horses—only six men all told—the chief of the band, called Running Bull Sheep, got on the bluff bigger than a wolf and demanded six horses. Well, that Texan wasn't looking for any particular Injun that day to give six of his own dear horses to. So we just drove on, paying no attention to Mr. Bull Sheep. About half a mile farther up the trail, the chief overtook us with all his bucks, and they were an ugly-looking lot. Well, this time he held up four fingers, meaning that four horses would be acceptable. But the Texan wasn't recognizing the Indian levy of taxation that year. When he refused them, the Indians never parleyed a moment, but set up a 'ki yi' and began circling round the herd on their ponies, Bull Sheep in the lead.

"As the chief passed the owner, his horse on a run, he gave a special shrill 'ki yi,' whipped a short carbine out of its scabbard, and shot twice into the rear of the herd. Never for a moment considering consequences, the Texan brought his six-shooter into action. It was a long, purty shot, and Mr. Bull Sheep threw his hands in the air and came off his horse backward, hard hit. This shooting in the rear of the horses gave them such a scare that we never checked them short of a mile. While the other Indians were holding a little powwow over their chief, we were making good time in the other direction, considering that we had over eight hundred loose horses. Fortunately our wagon and saddle horses had gone ahead that morning, but in the run we overtook them. As soon as we checked the herd from its scare, we turned them up the trail, stretched ropes from the wheels of the wagon, ran the saddle horses in, and changed mounts just a little quicker than I ever saw it done before or since. The cook had a saddle in the wagon, so we caught him up a horse, clapped leather on him, and tied him behind the wagon in case of an emergency. And you can just bet we changed to our best horses. When we overtook the herd, we were at least a mile and a half from where the shooting occurred, and there was no Indian in sight, but we felt that they hadn't given it up. We hadn't long to wait, though we would have waited willingly, before we heard their yells and saw the dust rising in clouds behind us. We quit the herd and wagon right there and rode for a swell of ground ahead that would give us a rear view of the scenery. The first view we caught of them was not very encouraging. They were riding after us like fiends and kicking up a dust like a windstorm. We had nothing but six-shooters, no good for long range. The owner of the horses admitted that it was useless to try to save the herd now, and if our scalps were worth saving it was high time to make ourselves scarce.

"Cantonment was a government post about twenty-five miles away, so we rode for it. Our horses were good Spanish stock, and the Indians' little bench-legged ponies were no match for them. But not satisfied with the wagon and herd falling into their hands, they followed us until we were within sight of the post. As hard luck would have it, the cavalry stationed at this post were off on some escort duty, and the infantry were useless in this case. When the cavalry returned a few days later, they tried to round up those Indians, and the Indian agent used his influence, but the horses were so divided up and scattered that they were never recovered."

"And did the man lose his horses entirely?" asked Flood, who had anteed up his last bean and joined us.

"He did. There was, I remember, a tinhorn lawyer up about Dodge who thought he could recover their value, as these were agency Indians and the government owed them money. But all I got for three months' wages due me was the horse I got away on."

A Lecture in Dodge City

told by
Fox Quarternight

There was much to be seen in Dodge, and as losing a night's sleep on duty was considered nothing, in hilarious recreation sleep would be entirely forgotten. McCann had not forgotten us, but had smuggled out a quart bottle to cut the alkali in our drinking water. But a quart amongst eight of us was not dangerous, so the night passed without incident, though we felt a growing impatience to get into town. As we expected, about sunrise the next morning our men off on holiday rode into camp, having never closed an eye during the entire night. They brought word from Flood that the herd would only graze over to Saw Log Creek that day, so as to let the remainder of us have a day and night in town. Lovell would only advance half a month's wages—twenty-five dollars—to the man. It was ample for any personal needs, though we had nearly three months' wages due, and no one protested, for the old man was generally right in his decisions. According to their report the boys had had a hog-killing time, old man Don having been out with them all night. It seems that McNulta stood in well with a class of practical jokers which included the officials of the town, and whenever there was anything on the tapis, he always got the word for himself and friends. During breakfast Fox Quarternight told this incident of the evening.

"Some professor, a professor in the occult sciences I think he called himself, had written to the mayor to know what kind of a point Dodge would be for a lecture. The lecture was to be free, but he also intimated that he had a card or two on the side up his sleeve, by which he expected to graft onto some of the coin of the realm from the wayfaring man as well as the citizen. The mayor turned the letter over to Bat Masterson, the city marshal, who answered it, and invited the professor to come on, assuring him that he was deeply interested in the occult sciences, personally, and would take pleasure in securing him a hall and a date, besides announcing his coming through the papers.

"Well, he was billed to deliver his lecture last night. Those old longhorns, McNulta and Lovell, got us in with the crowd, and while they didn't know exactly what was coming, they assured us that we couldn't afford to miss it. Well, at the appointed hour in the evening, the hall was packed, not over half being able to find seats. It is safe to say there were over five hundred men present, as it was announced for 'men only.' Every gambler in town was there, with a fair sprinkling of cowmen and our tribe. At the appointed hour, Masterson, as chairman, rapped for order, and in a neat little speech announced the object of the meeting. Bat mentioned the lack of interest in the West in the higher arts and sciences, and bespoke our careful attention to the subject under consideration for the evening. He said he felt it hardly necessary to urge the importance of good order, but if anyone had come out of idle curiosity or bent on mischief, as chairman of the meeting and a peace officer of the city, he would certainly brook no interruption. After a few other appropriate remarks, he introduced the speaker as Dr. J. Graves-Brown, the noted scientist.

"The professor was an oily-tongued fellow, and led off on the prelude to his lecture, while the audience was as quiet as mice and as grave as owls. After he had spoken about five minutes and was getting warmed up to his subject, he made an assertion which sounded a little fishy, and someone back in the audience blurted out, 'That's a damned lie.' The speaker halted in his discourse and looked at Masterson, who arose, and, drawing two six-shooters, looked the audience over as if trying to locate the offender. Laying the guns down on the table, he informed the meeting that another interruption would cost the offender his life, if he had to follow him to the Rio Grande or the British possessions. He then asked the professor, as there would be no further interruptions, to proceed with his lecture. The professor hesitated about going on, when Masterson assured him that it was evident that his audience, with the exception of one skulking coyote, was deeply interested in the subject, but that no one man could interfere with the freedom of speech in Dodge as long as it was a free country and he was city marshal. After this little talk, the speaker braced up and launched out again on his lecture. When he was once more under good headway, he had occasion to relate an exhibition which he had witnessed while studying his profession in India. The incident related was a trifle rank for anyone to swallow raw, when the same party who had interrupted before sang out, 'That's another damned lie.'

"Masterson came to his feet like a flash, a gun in each hand, saying, 'Stand up, you measly skunk, so I can see you.' Half a dozen men rose in different parts of the house and cut loose at him, and as they did so the lights went out and the room filled with smoke. Masterson was blazing away with two guns, which so lighted up the rostrum that we could see the professor crouching under the table. Of course, they were using blank cartridges, but the audience raised the long yell and poured out through the windows and doors, and the lecture was over. A couple of police came in later, so McNulta said, escorted the professor to his room in the hotel, and quietly advised him that Dodge was hardly capable of appreciating anything so advanced as a lecture on the occult sciences."

Revisiting the Old States

told by
Joe Stallings

After supper, while we were catching up our night horses, Flood said to us, "Now, boys, I'm going to leave the outfit and herd under Joe Stallings as *segundo*. It's hardly necessary to leave you under anyone as foreman, for you all know your places. But someone must be made responsible, and one bad boss will do less harm than half a dozen that mightn't agree. So you can put Honeyman on guard in your place at night, Joe, if you don't want to stand your own watch. Now behave yourselves, and when I meet you on the Republican, I'll bring out a box of cigars and have it charged up as axle grease when we get supplies at Ogallala. And don't sit up all night telling fool stories."

Our campfire that night was a good one, and in the absence of Flood, no one felt like going to bed until drowsiness compelled us. So we lounged around the fire smoking the hours away, and in spite of the admonition of our foreman, told stories far into the night. During the early portion of the evening, dog stories occupied the boards. As the evening wore on, the subject of revisiting the old states came up for discussion.

"You all talk about going back to the old states," said Joe Stallings, "but I don't take very friendly to the idea. I felt that way once and went home to Tennessee; but I want to tell you that after you live a few years in the sunny Southwest and get onto her ways, you can't stand it back there like you think you can. Now, when I went back, and I reckon my relations will average up pretty well—fought in the Confederate army, vote the Democratic ticket, and belong to the Methodist Church—they all seemed to be rapidly getting locoed. Why, my uncles, when they think of planting the old buck field or the widow's acre into any crop, they first go projecting around in the soil, and, as they say, analyze it, to see what kind of fertilizer it will require to produce the best results. Back there if one man raises ten acres of corn and his neighbor raises twelve, the one raising twelve is sure to look upon the other as though he lacked enterprise or had modest ambitions. Now, up around that old cow town, Abilene, Kansas, it's a common sight to see the cornfields stretch out like an ocean.

"And then their stock—they are all locoed about that. Why, I know people who will pay a hundred dollars for siring a colt, and if there's one drop of mongrel blood in that sire's veins for ten generations back on either side of his ancestral tree, it condemns him, though he may be a good horse otherwise. They are strong on standard-bred horses; but as for me, my mount is all right. I wouldn't trade with any man in this outfit, without it would be Flood, and there's none of them standard-bred either. Why, shucks, if you had the pick of all the standard-bred horses in Tennessee, you couldn't handle a herd of cattle like ours with them, without carrying a commissary with you to feed them. No; they would never fit here—it takes a range-raised horse to run cattle; one that can rustle and live on grass.

"Another thing about those people back in those old states. Not one in ten, I'll gamble, knows the teacher he sends his children to school to. But when he has a promising colt to be shod, the owner goes to the blacksmith shop himself, and he and the smith will sit on the back sill of the shop, and they will discuss how to shoe that filly so as to give her certain knee action which she seems to need. Probably, says one, a little weight on her toe would give her reach. And there they will sit and pow-wow and make medicine for an hour or two. And while the blacksmith is shoeing her, the owner will tell him in confidence what a wonderful burst of speed she developed yesterday, while he was speeding her on the back stretch. And then just as he turned her into the home stretch, she threw a shoe and he had to check her in; but if there'd been anyone to catch her time, he was certain it was better than a two-ten clip. And that same colt, you couldn't cut a lame cow out of the shade of a tree on her.

"A man back there—he's rich, too, though his father made it—gave a thousand dollars for a pair of dogs before they were born. The terms were one half cash and the balance when they were old enough to ship to him. And for fear they were not the proper mustard, he had that dog man sue him in court for the balance, so as to make him prove the pedigree. Now Bob, there, thinks that old hound of his is the real stuff, but he wouldn't do now; almost every year the style changes in dogs back in the old states. One year maybe it's a little white dog with red eyes, and the very next it's a long bench-legged black dog with a Dutch name that right now I disremember. Common old pot hounds and everyday yellow dogs have gone out of style entirely. No, you can all go back that want to, but as long as I can hold a job with Lovell and Flood, I'll try and worry along in my own way."

On finishing his little yarn, Stallings arose, saying, "I must take a listen to my men on herd. It always frets me for fear my men will ride too near the cattle."

A minute later he called us, and when several of us walked out to where he was listening, we recognized Roundtree's voice, singing—

Little black bull came down the hillside,

Down the hillside, down the hillside,
Little black bull came down the hillside,
Long time ago.

"Whenever my men sing that song on guard, it tells me that everything is amply serene," remarked our *segundo,* with the air of a field marshal, as we walked back to the fire.

Bear-Sign Artist

told by
John Officer

In order to avoid listening to the gloomy tales that were being narrated around the campfire, a number of us got up and went out as if to look up the night horses on picket. The Rebel and I pulled our picket pins and changed our horses to fresh grazing, and after lying down among the horses, out of hearing of the camp, for over an hour, returned to the wagon expecting to retire.

A number of the boys were making down their beds, as it was already late; but on our arrival at the fire one of the boys had just concluded a story, as gloomy as the others which had preceded it.

"These stories you are all telling tonight," said Flood, "remind me of what Lige Link said to the book agent when he was shearing sheep. 'I reckon,' said Lige, 'that book of yours has a heap sight more poetry in it than there is in shearing sheep.' I wish I had gone on guard tonight, so I could have missed these stories."

At this juncture the first guard rode in, having been relieved, and John Officer, who had exchanged places on guard that night with Moss Strayhorn, remarked that the cattle were uneasy.

"This outfit," said he, "didn't half water the herd today. One third of them hasn't bedded down yet, and they don't act as if they aim to, either. There's no excuse for it in a well-watered country like this. I'll leave the saddle on my horse, anyhow."

"Now that's the result," said our foreman, "of the hour we spent around the grave today, when we ought to have been tending to our job. This outfit," he continued, when Officer returned from picketing his horse, "have been trying to hold funeral services over that Pierce man's grave back there. You'd think so, anyway, from the tales they've been telling. I hope you won't get the sniffles and tell any."

"This letting yourself get gloomy," said Officer, "reminds me of a time we once had at the J H camp in Cherokee Strip. It was near Christmas, and the work was all done up. The boys had blowed in their summer's wages and were feeling glum all over. One or two of the boys were lamenting that they hadn't gone home to see the old folks. This gloomy feeling kept spreading until they actually wouldn't speak to each other. One of them would go out and sit on the woodpile for hours, all by himself, and make a new set of good resolutions. Another would go out and sit on the ground, on the sunny side of the corrals, and dig holes in the frozen earth with his knife. They wouldn't come to meals when the cook called them.

"Now, Miller, the foreman, didn't have any sympathy for them; in fact he delighted to see them in that condition. He hadn't any use for a man who wasn't dead tough under any condition. I've known him to camp his outfit on alkali water, so the men would get out in the morning, and every rascal beg leave to ride on the outside circle on the morning roundup. Well, three days before Christmas, just when things were looking gloomiest, there drifted up from the Cheyenne country one of the old-timers. None of them had seen him in four years, though he had worked on that range before, and with the exception of myself, they all knew him. He was riding the chuckline all right, but Miller gave him a welcome, as he was the real thing. He had been working out in the Panhandle country, New Mexico, and the devil knows where, since he had left that range. He was meaty with news and scary stories. The boys would sit around and listen to him yarn, and now and then a smile would come on their faces. Miller was delighted with his guest. He had shown no signs of letting up at eleven o'clock the first night, when he happened to mention where he was the Christmas before.

" 'There was a little woman at the ranch,' said he, 'wife of the owner, and I was helping her get up dinner, as we had quite a number of folks at the ranch. She asked me to make the bear sign—doughnuts, she called them—and I did, though she had to show me how some little. Well, fellows, you ought to have seen them—just sweet enough, browned to a turn, and enough to last a week. All the folks at dinner that day praised them. Since then, I've had a chance to try my hand several times, and you may not tumble to the diversity of all my accomplishments, but I'm an artist on bear sign.'

"Miller arose, took him by the hand, and said, 'That's straight, now, is it?'

" 'That's straight. Making bear sign is my long suit.'

" 'Mouse,' said Miller to one of the boys, 'go out and bring in his saddle from the stable and put it under my bed. Throw his horse in the big pasture in the morning. He stays here until spring; and the first spear of green grass I see, his name goes on the payroll. This outfit is shy on men who can make bear sign. Now, I was thinking that you could spread down your blankets on the hearth, but you can sleep with me tonight. You go to work on this specialty of yours right after breakfast in the morning, and show us what you can do in that line.'

"They talked quite a while longer, and then turned in for the night. The next morning after breakfast was over, he got the needed articles together and went to work. But there was a surprise in store for him. There was nearly a dozen men lying around, all able eaters. By ten o'clock he began to turn them out as he said he could. When the regular cook had to have the stove to get dinner, the taste which we had had made us ravenous for more. Dinner over, he went at them again in earnest. A boy riding towards the railroad with an important letter dropped in, and as he claimed he could only stop for a moment, we stood aside until he had had a taste, though he filled himself like a poisoned pup. After eating a solid hour, he filled his pockets and rode away. One of our regular men called after him, 'Don't tell anybody what we got.'

"We didn't get any supper that night. Not a man could have eaten a bite. Miller made him knock off along in the shank of the evening, as he had done enough for any one day. The next morning after breakfast he fell to at the bear sign once more. Miller rolled a barrel of flour into the kitchen from the storehouse, and told him to fly at them. 'About how many do you think you'll want?' asked our bear-sign man.

"'That big tub full won't be too many,' answered Miller. 'Some of these fellows haven't had any of this kind of truck since they were little boys. If this gets out, I look for men from other camps.'

"The fellow fell to his work like a thoroughbred, which he surely was. About ten o'clock two men rode up from a camp to the north, which the boy had passed the day before with the letter. They never went near the dugout, but straight to the kitchen. That movement showed that they were on to the racket. An hour later old Tom Cave rode in, his horse all in a lather, all the way from Garretson's camp, twenty-five miles to the east. The old sinner said that he had been on the frontier some little time, and that they were the best bear sign he had tasted in forty years. He refused to take a stool and sit down like civilized folks, but stood up by the tub and picked out the ones which were a pale brown.

"After dinner our man threw off his overshirt, unbuttoned his red undershirt and turned it in until you could see the hair on his breast. Rolling up his sleeves, he flew at his job once more. He was getting his work reduced to a science by this time. He rolled his dough, cut his dough, and turned out the fine brown bear sign to the satisfaction of all.

"His capacity, however, was limited. About two o'clock Doc Langford and two of his peelers were seen riding up. When he came into the kitchen, Doc swore by all that was good and holy that he hadn't heard that our artist had come back to that country. But anyone that was noticing could see him edge around to the tub. It was easy to see that he was lying. This luck of ours was circulating faster than a secret amongst women. Our man, though, stood at his post like the boy on the burning deck. When night came on, he hadn't covered the bottom of the tub. When he knocked off, Doc Langford and his men gobbled up what was left. We gave them a mean look as they rode off, but they came back the next day, five strong. Our regular men around camp didn't like it, the way things were going. They tried to act polite to—"

"Calling bear sign doughnuts," interrupted Quince Forrest, "reminds me what—"

"Will you kindly hobble your lip," said Officer; "I have the floor at present. As I was saying, they tried to act polite to company that way, but we hadn't got a smell the second day. Our man showed no signs of fatigue, and told several good stories that night. He was tough. The next day was Christmas, but he had no respect for a holiday, and made up a large batch of dough before breakfast. It was a good thing he did, for early that morning 'Original' John Smith and four of his peelers rode in from the west, their horses all covered with frost. They must have started at daybreak—it was a good twenty-two-mile ride. They wanted us to believe that they had simply come over to spend Christmas with us. Company that way, you can't say anything. But the easy manner in which they gravitated around that tub—not even waiting to be invited—told a different tale. They were not nearly satisfied by noon.

"Then who should come drifting in as we were sitting down to dinner but Billy Dunlap and Jim Hale from Quinlin's camp, thirty miles south on the Cimarron. Dunlap always holed up like a bear in the winter, and several of the boys spilled their coffee at sight of him. He put up a thin excuse just like the rest. Anyone could see through it. But there it was again—he was company. Lots of us had eaten at his camp and complained of his chuck; therefore, we were nice to him. Miller called our man out behind the kitchen and told him to knock off if he wanted to. But he wouldn't do it. He was clean strain—I'm not talking. Dunlap ate hardly any dinner, we noticed, and the very first batch of bear sign turned out, he loads up a tin plate and goes out and sits behind the storehouse in the sun, all alone in his glory. He satisfied himself out of the tub after that.

"He and Hale stayed all night, and Dunlap kept everyone awake with the nightmare. Yes, kept fighting the demons all night. The next morning Miller told him that he was surprised that an old gray-haired man like him didn't know when he had enough, but must gorge himself like some silly kid. Miller told him that he was welcome to stay a week if he wanted to, but he would have to sleep in the stable. It was cruel to the horses, but the men were entitled to a little sleep, at least in the winter. Miller tempered his remarks with all kindness, and Dunlap acted as if he was sorry, and as good as admitted that his years were telling on him. That day our man filled his tub. He was simply an artist on bear sign."

"Calling bear sign doughnuts," cut in Quince Forrest again, as soon as he saw an opening, "reminds me what the little boy said who went—"

But there came a rumbling of many hoofs from the bed-ground. "There's hell for you," said half a dozen men in a chorus, and every man in camp ran for his horse but the cook, and he climbed into the wagon. The roar of the running cattle was like approaching thunder, but the flash from the six-shooters of the men on guard indicated they were quartering by camp, heading out towards the hills. Horses became so excited they were difficult to bridle. There was plenty of earnest and sincere swearing done that night. All the fine sentiment and melancholy of the hour previous vanished in a moment, as the men threw themselves into their saddles, riding deep, for it was uncertain footing to horses.

Within two minutes from the time the herd left the

bed-ground, fourteen of us rode on their left point and across their front, firing our six-shooters in their faces. By the time the herd had covered a scant mile, we had thrown them into a mill. They had run so compactly that there were no stragglers, so we loosened out and gave them room; but it was a long time before they relaxed any, but continued going round and round like a water wheel or an endless chain. The foreman ordered three men on the heaviest horses to split them. The men rode out a short distance to get the required momentum, wheeled their horses, and, wedge-shaped, struck this sea of cattle and entered, but it instantly closed in their wake as though it had been water. For an hour they rode through the herd, back and forth, now from this quarter, now from that, and finally the mill was broken. After midnight, as luck would have it, heavy dark clouds banked in the northwest, and lightning flashed, and before a single animal had lain down, a drizzling rain set in. That settled it; it was an all-night job now. We drifted about hither and yon. Horses, men, and cattle turned their backs to the wind and rain and waited for morning. We were so familiar with the signs of coming day that we turned them loose half an hour before dawn, leaving herders, and rode for camp.

Miss Precilla June Jones

told by
Bob Blades

Our visitors interested us, for it is probable that not a man in our outfit had ever seen a miner before, though we had read of the life and were deeply interested in everything they did or said. They were very plain men and of simple manners, but we had great difficulty in getting them to talk. After supper, while idling away a couple of hours around our campfire, the outfit told stories, in the hope that our guests would become reminiscent and give us some insight into their experiences, Bob Blades leading off.

"I was in a cow town once up on the head of the Chisholm Trail at a time when a church fair was being pulled off. There were lots of old longhorn cowmen living in the town, who owned cattle in that Cherokee Strip that Officer is always talking about. Well, there's lots of folks up there that think a nigger is as good as anybody else, and when you find such people set in their ways, it's best not to argue matters with them, but lay low and let on you think that way too. That's the way those old Texas cowmen acted about it.

"Well, at this church fair there was to be voted a prize of a nice baby wagon, which had been donated by some merchant, to the prettiest baby under a year old. Colonel Bob Zellers was in town at the time, stopping at a hotel where the darky cook was a man who had once worked for him on the trail. Frog, the darky, had married when he quit the Colonel's service, and at the time of this fair there was a pickaninny in his family about a year old, and nearly the color of a new saddle. A few of these old cowmen got funny and thought it would be a good joke to have Frog enter his baby at the fair, and Colonel Bob being the leader in the movement, he had no trouble convincing the darky that that baby wagon was his, if he would only enter his youngster. Frog thought the world of the old Colonel, and the latter assured him that he would vote for his baby while he had a dollar or a cow left. The result was, Frog gave his enthusiastic consent, and the Colonel agreed to enter the pickaninny in the contest.

"Well, the Colonel attended to the entering of the baby's name, and then on the dead quiet went around and rustled up every cowman and puncher in town, and had them promise to be on hand, to vote for the prettiest baby at ten cents a throw. The fair was being held in the largest hall in town, and at the appointed hour we were all on hand, as well as Frog and his wife and baby. There were about a dozen entries, and only one blackbird in the covey. The list of contestants was read by the minister, and as each name was announced, there was a vigorous clapping of hands all over the house by the friends of each baby. But when the name of Miss Precilla June Jones was announced, the Texas contingent made their presence known by such a deafening outburst of applause that old Frog grinned from ear to ear—he saw himself right then pushing that baby wagon.

"Well, on the first heat we voted sparingly, and as the vote was read out about every quarter hour, Precilla June Jones on the first turn was fourth in the race. On the second report, our favorite had moved up to third place, after which the weaker ones were deserted, and all the voting blood was centered on the two white leaders, with our blackbird a close third. We were behaving ourselves nicely, and our money was welcome if we weren't. When the third vote was announced, Frog's pickaninny was second in the race, with her nose lapped on the flank of the leader. Then those who thought a darky was as good as anyone else got on the prod in a mild form, and you could hear them voicing their opinions all over the hall. We heard it all, but sat as nice as pie and never said a word.

"When the final vote was called for, we knew it was the home stretch, and every rascal of us got his weasel skin out and sweetened the voting on Miss Precilla June Jones. Some of those old longhorns didn't think any more of a twenty-dollar gold piece than I do of a white chip, especially when there was a chance to give those good people a dose of their own medicine. I don't know how many votes we cast on the last whirl, but we swamped all opposition, and our favorite cantered under the wire an easy winner. Then you should have heard the kicking, but we kept still and inwardly chuckled. The minister announced the winner, and some of those good people didn't have any better manners than to hiss and cut up ugly. We stayed until Frog got the new baby wagon in his clutches, when we dropped out casually and met at the Ranch saloon, where Colonel Zellers had taken possession behind the bar and was dispensing hospitality in proper celebration of his victory."

Much to our disappointment, our guests remained silent and showed no disposition to talk, except to answer civil questions which Flood asked regarding the trail crossing on the Missouri, and what that river was like in the vicinity of old Fort Benton. When the questions had been answered, they again relapsed into silence.

The Black-Waxy near Waxahachie

told by
Joe Stallings

The fire was replenished, and after the conversation had touched on several subjects, Joe Stallings took his turn with a yarn.

"When my folks first came to Texas," said Joe, "they settled in Ellis County, near Waxahachie. My father was one of the pioneers in that county at a time when his nearest neighbor lived ten miles from his front gate. But after the war, when the country had settled up, these old pioneers naturally hung together and visited and chummed with one another in preference to the new settlers. One spring when I was about fifteen years old, one of those old pioneer neighbors of ours died, and my father decided that he would go to the funeral or burst a hamstring. If any of you know anything about that black-waxy, hog-wallow land in Ellis County, you know that when it gets muddy in the spring a wagon wheel will fill solid with waxy mud. So at the time of this funeral it was impossible to go on the road with any kind of a vehicle, and my father had to go on horseback. He was an old man at the time and didn't like the idea, but it was either go on horseback or stay at home, and go he would.

"They raise good horses in Ellis County, and my father had raised some of the best of them—brought the stock from Tennessee. He liked good blood in a horse, and was always opposed to racing, but he raised some boys who weren't. I had a number of brothers older than myself, and they took a special pride in trying every colt we raised, to see what he amounted to in speed. Of course, this had to be done away from home; but that was easy, for these older brothers thought nothing of riding twenty miles to a tournament, barbecue, or roundup, and when away from home they always tried their horses with the best in the country. At the time of this funeral, we had a crackerjack five-year-old chestnut sorrel gelding that could show his heels to any horse in the country. He was a peach—you could turn him on a saddle blanket and jump him fifteen feet, and that cow never lived that he couldn't cut.

"So the day of the funeral my father was in a quandary as to which horse to ride, but when he appealed to his boys, they recommended the best on the ranch, which was the chestnut gelding. My old man had some doubts as to his ability to ride the horse, for he hadn't been on a horse's back for years; but my brothers assured him that the chestnut was as obedient as a kitten, and that before he had been on the road an hour the mud would take all the frisk and frolic out of him. There was nearly fifteen miles to go, and they assured him that he would never get there if he rode any other horse. Well, at last he consented to ride the gelding, and the horse was made ready, properly groomed, his tail tied up, and saddled and led up to the block. It took every member of the family to get my father rigged to start, but at last he announced himself as ready. Two of my brothers held the horse until he found the off stirrup, and then they turned him loose. The chestnut danced off a few rods, and settled down into a steady clip that was good for five or six miles an hour.

"My father reached the house in good time for the funeral services, but when the procession started for the burial ground, the horse was somewhat restless and impatient from the cold. There was quite a string of wagons and other vehicles from the immediate neighborhood which had braved the mud, and the line was nearly half a mile in length between the house and the graveyard. There were also possibly a hundred men on horseback bringing up the rear of the procession; and the chestnut, not understanding the solemnity of the occasion, was right on his mettle. Surrounded as he was by other horses, he kept his weather eye open for a race, for in coming home from dances and picnics with my brothers, he had often been tried in short dashes of half a mile or so. In order to get him out of the crowd of horses, my father dropped back with another pioneer to the extreme rear of the funeral line.

"When the procession was nearing the cemetery, a number of horsemen who were late galloped up in the rear. The chestnut, supposing a race was on, took the bit in his teeth and tore down past the procession as though it was a free-for-all Texas sweepstakes, the old man's white beard whipping the breeze in his endeavor to hold in the horse. Nor did he check him until the head of the procession had been passed. When my father returned home that night, there was a family roundup, for he was smoking under the collar. Of course, my brothers denied having ever run the horse, and my mother took their part; but the old gent knew a thing or two about horses, and shortly afterwards he got even with his boys by selling the chestnut, which broke their hearts properly."

The Cat in the Jacal

told by
Aaron Scales

We made camp on the outskirts of the timber, and at early dusk great flocks of pigeons began to arrive at their roosting place. We only had four shotguns, and, dividing into pairs, we entered the roost shortly after dark. Glenn Gallup fell to me as my pardner. I carried the gunny sack for the birds, not caring for a gun in such unfair shooting. The flights continued to arrive for fully an hour after we entered the roost, and in half a dozen shots we bagged over fifty birds. Remembering the admonition of Uncle Lance, Gallup refused to kill more, and we sat down and listened to the rumbling noises of the grove. There was a constant chattering of the pigeons, and as they settled in great flights in the trees overhead, whipping the branches with their wings in search of footing, they frequently fell to the ground at our feet.

Gallup and I returned to camp early. Before we had skinned our kill the others had all come in, disgusted with the ease with which they had filled their bags. We soon had two pots filled and on the fire parboiling, while Tiburcio lined two ovens with pastry, all ready for the baking. In a short time two horsemen, attracted by our fire, crossed the river below our camp and rode up.

"Hello, Uncle Lance," lustily shouted one of them, as he dismounted. "It's you, is it, that's shooting my pigeons? All right, sir, I'll stay all night and help you eat them. I had figured on riding back to the Frio to-night, but I've changed my mind. Got any horse hobbles here?" The two men, George Nathan and Hugh Trotter, were accommodated with hobbles, and after an exchange of commonplace news of the country, we settled down to storytelling. Trotter was a convivial acquaintance of Aaron Scales, quite a vagabond and consequently a storyteller. After Trotter had narrated a late dream, Scales unlimbered and told one of his own.

"I remember a dream I had several years ago, and the only way I can account for it was, I had been drinking more or less during the day. I dreamt I was making a long ride across a dreary desert, and towards night it threatened a bad storm. I began to look around for some shelter. I could just see the tops of a clump of trees beyond a hill, and rode hard to get to them, thinking that there might be a house amongst them. How I did ride! But I certainly must have had a poor horse, for I never seemed to get any nearer that timber. I rode and rode, but all this time, hours and hours it seemed, and the storm gathering and scattering raindrops falling, the timber seemed scarcely any nearer.

"At last I managed to reach the crest of the hill. Well, sir, there wasn't a tree in sight, only, under the brow of the hill, a deserted adobe jacal, and I rode for that, picketed my horse and went in. The jacal had a thatched roof with several large holes in it, and in the fireplace burned a roaring fire. That was some strange, but I didn't mind it and I was warming my hands before the fire and congratulating myself on my good luck, when a large black cat sprang from the outside into an open window, and said, 'Pardner, it looks like a bad night outside.'

"I eyed him a little suspiciously; but, for all that, if he hadn't spoken, I wouldn't have thought anything about it, for I like cats. He walked backward and forward on the window sill, his spine and tail nicely arched, and rubbed himself on either window jamb. I watched him some little time, and finally concluded to make friends with him. Going over to the window, I put out my hand to stroke his glossy back, when a gust of rain came through the window and the cat vanished into the darkness.

"I went back to the fire, pitying the cat out there in the night's storm, and was really sorry I had disturbed him. I didn't give the matter overmuch attention but sat before the fire, wondering who could have built it and listening to the rain outside, when all of a sudden Mr. Cat walked between my legs, rubbing himself against my boots, purring and singing. Once or twice I thought of stroking his fur, but checked myself on remembering he had spoken to me on the window sill. He would walk over and rub himself against the jambs of the fireplace, and then come back and rub himself against my boots friendly like. I saw him just as clear as I see those pots on the fire or these saddles lying around here. I was noting every move of his as he meandered around, when presently he cocked up an eye at me and remarked, 'Old sport, this is a fine fire we have here.'

"I was beginning to feel a little creepy, for I'd seen mad dogs and skunks, and they say a cat gets locoed likewise, and the cuss was talking so cleverly that I began to lose my regard for him. After a little while I concluded to pet him, for he didn't seem a bit afraid; but as I put out my hand to catch him, he nimbly hopped into the roaring fire and vanished. Then I did feel foolish. I had a good six-shooter, and made up my mind if he showed up again I'd plug him one for luck. I was growing sleepy, and it was getting late, so I concluded to spread down my saddle blankets and slicker before the fire and go to sleep. While I was making down my bed, I happened to look towards the fire, when there was my black cat, with not even a hair singed. I drew my gun quietly and cracked away at him, when he let out the funniest little laugh, saying, 'You've been drinking, Aaron; you're nervous; you couldn't hit a flock of barns.'

"I was getting excited by this time, and cut loose on him rapidly, but he dodged every shot, jumping from the hearth to the mantel, from the mantel to an old table, from there to a niche in the wall, and from the niche clear across the room and out of the window. About then I was some nervous, and after a while lay down before the fire and tried to go to sleep.

"It was a terrible night outside—one of those nights when you can hear things; and with the vivid imagination I was enjoying then, I was almost afraid to try to sleep. But just as I was going into a doze, I raised up my head, and there was my cat walking up and down my frame, his back arched and his tail flirting with the slow sinuous movement of a snake. I reached for my gun, and as it clicked in cocking, he began raking my legs, sharpening his claws and growling like a tiger. I gave a yell and kicked him off, when he sprang up on the old table and I could see his eyes glaring at me. I emptied my gun at him a second time, and at every shot he crouched lower and crept forward as if getting ready to spring. When I had fired the last shot I jumped up and ran out into the rain, and hadn't gone more than a hundred yards before I fell into a dry wash. When I crawled out there was that d——d cat rubbing himself against my bootleg. I stood breathless for a minute, thinking what next to do, and the cat remarked, 'Wasn't that a peach of a race we just had!'

"I made one or two vicious kicks at him and he again vanished. Well, fellows, in that dream I walked around that old jacal all night in my shirt sleeves, and it raining pitchforks. A number of times I peeped in through the window or door, and there sat the cat on the hearth, in full possession of the shack, and me out in the weather. Once when I looked in he was missing, but while I was watching he sprang through a hole in the roof, alighting in the fire, from which he walked out gingerly, shaking his feet as if he had just been out in the wet. I shot away every cartridge I had at him, but in the middle of the shooting he would just coil up before the fire and snooze away.

"That night was an eternity of torment to me, and I was relieved when someone knocked on the door, and I awoke to find myself in a good bed and pounding my ear on a goose-hair pillow in a hotel in Oakville. Why, I wouldn't have another dream like that for a half interest in the Las Palomas brand. No, honest, if I thought drinking gave me that hideous dream, here would be one lad ripe for reform."

"It strikes me," said Uncle Lance, rising and lifting a pot lid, "that these birds are parboiled by this time. Bring me a fork, Enrique. Well, I should say they were. I hope hell ain't any hotter than that fire. Now, Tiburcio, if you have everything ready, we'll put them in the oven, and bake them a couple of hours."

Trotter's Sack of Salt

told by
Hugh Trotter

Several of us assisted in fixing the fire and properly coaling the ovens. When this had been attended to, and we had again resumed our easy positions around the fire, Trotter began a yarn.

''Aaron, you ought to cut drinking out of your amusements; you haven't the constitution to stand it. Now with me it's different. I can drink a week and never sleep; that's the kind of build to have if you expect to travel and meet all comers. Last year I was working for a Kansas City man on the trail, and after the cattle were delivered about a hundred miles beyond—Ellsworth, up in Kansas—he sent us home by way of Kansas City. In fact, that was about the only route we could take. Well, it was a successful trip, and as this man was plumb white, anyhow, he concluded to show us the sights around his burg. He was interested in a commission firm out at the stockyards, and the night we reached there all the office men, including the old man himself, turned themselves loose to show us a good time.

"We had been drinking alkali water all summer, and along about midnight they began to drop out until there was no one left to face the music except a little cattle salesman and myself. After all the others quit us, we went into a feed trough on a back street, and had a good supper. I had been drinking everything like a good fellow, and at several places there was no salt to put in the beer. The idea struck me that I would buy a sack of salt from this eating ranch and take it with me. The landlord gave me a funny look, but after some little parley went to the rear and brought out a five-pound sack of table salt.

"It was just what I wanted, and after paying for it the salesman and I started out to make a night of it. This yardman was a short, fat Dutchman, and we made a team for your whiskers. I carried the sack of salt under my arm, and the quantity of beer we killed before daylight was a caution. About daybreak, the salesman wanted me to go to our hotel and go to bed, but as I never drink and sleep at the same time, I declined. Finally he explained to me that he would have to be at the yards at eight o'clock, and begged me to excuse him. By this time he was several sheets in the wind, while I could walk a chalk line without a waver. Somehow we drifted around to the hotel where the outfit were supposed to be stopping, and lined up at the bar for a final drink. It was just daybreak, and between that Dutch cattle salesman and the barkeeper and myself, it would have taken a bookkeeper to have kept a check on the drinks we consumed—every one the last.

"Then the Dutchman gave me the slip and was gone, and I wandered into the office of the hotel. A newsboy sold me a paper, and the next minute a bootblack wanted to give me a shine. Well, I took a seat for a shine, and for two hours I sat there as full as a tick, and as dignified as a judge on the bench. All the newsboys and bootblacks caught on, and before any of the outfit showed up that morning to rescue me, I had bought a dozen papers and had my boots shined for the tenth time. If I'd been foxy enough to have got rid of that sack of salt, no one could have told I was off the reservation; but there it was under my arm. If ever I make another trip over the trail, and touch at Kansas City returning, I'll hunt up that cattle salesman, for he's the only man I ever met that can pace in my class."

"Did you hear that tree break a few minutes ago?" inquired Mr. Nathan. "There goes another one. It hardly looks possible that enough pigeons could settle on a tree to break it down. Honestly, I'd give a purty to know how many birds are in that roost tonight. More than there are cattle in Texas, I'll bet. Why, Hugh killed, with both barrels, twenty-two at one shot."

Good for Two Drinks

told by
Glenn Gallup

We had brought blankets along, but it was early and no one thought of sleeping for an hour yet. Mr. Nathan was quite a sportsman, and after he and Uncle Lance had discussed the safest method of hunting javelina, it again devolved on the boys to entertain the party with stories.

"I was working on a ranch once," said Glenn Gallup, "out on the Concho River. It was a stag outfit, there being few women then out Concho way. One day two of the boys were riding in home when an accident occurred. They had been shooting more or less during the morning, and one of them, named Bill Cook, had carelessly left the hammer of his six-shooter on a cartridge. As Bill jumped his horse over a dry arroyo, his pistol was thrown from its holster, and, falling on the hard ground, was discharged. The bullet struck him in the ankle, ranged upward, shattering the large bone in his leg into fragments, and finally lodged in the saddle.

"They were about five miles from camp when the accident happened. After they realized how bad he was hurt, Bill remounted his horse and rode nearly a mile; but the wound bled so then that the fellow with him insisted on his getting off and lying on the ground while he went into the ranch for a wagon. Well, it's to be supposed that he lost no time riding in, and I was sent to San Angelo for a doctor. It was just noon when I got off. I had to ride thirty miles. Talk about your good horses—I had one that day. I took a free gait from the start, but the last ten miles was the fastest, for I covered the entire distance in less than three hours. There was a doctor in the town who'd been on the frontier all of his life, and was used to such calls. Well, before dark that evening we drove into the ranch.

"They had got the lad into the ranch, had checked the flow of blood and eased the pain by standing on a chair and pouring water on the wound from a height. But Bill looked pale as a ghost from the loss of blood. The doctor gave the leg a single look, and, turning to us, said, 'Boys, she has to come off.'

"The doctor talked to Bill freely and frankly, telling him that it was the only chance for his life. He readily consented to the operation, and while the doctor was getting him under the influence of opiates we fixed up an operating table. When all was ready, the doctor took the leg off below the knee, cursing us generally for being so sensitive to cutting and the sight of blood. There was quite a number of boys at the ranch, but it affected them all alike. It was interesting to watch him cut and tie arteries and saw the bones, and I think I stood it better than any of them. When the operation was over, we gave the fellow the best bed the ranch afforded and fixed him up comfortable. The doctor took the bloody stump and wrapped it up in an old newspaper, saying he would take it home with him.

"After supper the surgeon took a sleep, saying we would start back to town by two o'clock, so as to be there by daylight. He gave instructions to call him in case Bill awoke, but he hoped the boy would take a good sleep. As I had left my horse in town, I was expected to go back with him. Shortly after midnight the fellow awoke, so we aroused the doctor, who reported him doing well. The old Doc sat by his bed for an hour and told him all kinds of stories. He had been a surgeon in the Confederate army, and from the drift of his talk you'd think it was impossible to kill a man without cutting off his head.

" 'Now take a young fellow like you,' said the doctor to his patient; 'if he was all shot to pieces, just so the parts would hang together, I could fix him up and he would get well. You have no idea, son, how much lead a young man can carry.' We had coffee and lunch before starting, the doctor promising to send me back at once with necessary medicines.

"We had a very pleasant trip driving back to town that night. The stories he could tell were like a song with ninety verses, no two alike. It was hardly daybreak when we reached San Angelo, rustled out a sleepy hostler at the livery stable where the team belonged, and had the horses cared for; and as we left the stable the doctor gave me his instrument case, while he carried the amputated leg in the paper. We both felt the need of a bracer after our night's ride, so we looked around to see if any saloons were open. There was only one that showed any signs of life, and we headed for that. The doctor was in the lead as we entered, and we both knew the barkeeper well. This barkeeper was a practical joker himself, and he and the doctor were great hunting companions. We walked up to the bar together, when the doctor laid the package on the counter and asked, 'Is this good for two drinks?' The barkeeper, with a look of expectation in his face as if the package might contain half a dozen quail or some fresh fish, broke the string and unrolled it. Without a word he walked straight from behind the bar and out of the house. If he had been shot himself he couldn't have looked whiter.

"The doctor went behind the bar and said: 'Glenn, what are you going to take?'

" 'Let her come straight, doctor,' was my reply, and we both took the same. We had the house all to ourselves, and after a second round of drinks took our leave. As we left by the front door, we saw the barkeeper leaning against a hitching post half a block below.

"The doctor called to him as we were leaving, 'Billy, if the drinks ain't on you, charge them to me.' "

A Blue Bird Swooping Down like a Pigeon Hawk

told by
Theodore Quayle

The moon was just rising, and at Uncle Lance's suggestion we each carried in a turn of wood. Piling a portion of it on the fire, the blaze soon lighted up the camp, throwing shafts of light far into the recesses of the woods around us. "In another hour," said Uncle Lance, recoaling the oven lids, "that smaller pie will be all ready to serve, but we'll keep the big one for breakfast. So, boys, if you want to sit up awhile longer, we'll have a midnight lunch, and then all turn in for about forty winks." As the oven lid was removed from time to time to take note of the baking, savory odors of the pie were wafted to our anxious nostrils. On the intimation that one oven would be ready in an hour, not a man suggested blankets, and, taking advantage of the lull, Theodore Quayle claimed attention.

"Another fellow and myself," said Quayle, "were knocking around Fort Worth one time seeing the sights. We had drunk until it didn't taste right any longer. This chum of mine was queer in his drinking. If he ever got enough once, he didn't want any more for several days: you could cure him by offering him plenty. But with just the right amount on board, he was a hail fellow. He was a big, ambling, awkward cuss, who could be led into anything on a hint or suggestion. We had been knocking around the town for a week, until there was nothing new to be seen.

"Several times as we passed a millinery shop, kept by a little blonde, we had seen her standing at the door. Something—it might have been his ambling walk, but, anyway, something—about my chum amused her, for she smiled and watched him as we passed. He never could walk along beside you for any distance, but would trail behind and look into the windows. He could not be hurried—not in town. I mentioned to him that he had made a mash on the little blond milliner, and he at once insisted that I should show her to him. We passed down on the opposite side of the street and I pointed out the place. Then we walked by several times, and finally passed when she was standing in the doorway talking to some customers. As we came up he straightened himself, caught her eye, and tipped his hat with the politeness of a dancing master. She blushed to the roots of her hair, and he walked on very erect some little distance, then we turned a corner and held a confab. He was for playing the whole string, discount or no discount, anyway.

"An excuse to go in was wanting, but we thought we could invent one; however, he needed a drink or two to facilitate his thinking and loosen his tongue. To get them was easier than the excuse; but with the drinks the motive was born. 'You wait here,' said he to me, 'until I go round to the livery stable and get my coat off my saddle.' He never encumbered himself with extra clothing. We had not seen our horses, saddles, or any of our belongings during the week of our visit. When he returned he inquired, 'Do I need a shave?'

" 'Oh, no,' I said, 'you need no shave. You may have a drink too many, or lack one of having enough. It's hard to make a close calculation on you.'

" 'Then I'm all ready,' said he, 'for I've just the right gauge of steam.' He led the way as we entered. It was getting dark and the shop was empty of customers. Where he ever got the manners, heaven only knows. Once inside the door we halted, and she kept a counter between us as she approached. She ought to have called the police and had us run in. She was probably scared, but her voice was fairly steady as she spoke. 'Gentlemen, what can I do for you?'

" 'My friend here,' said he, with a bow and a wave of the hand, 'was unfortunate enough to lose a wager made between us. The terms of the bet were that the loser was to buy a new hat for one of the dining-room girls at our hotel. As we are leaving town tomorrow, we have just dropped in to see if you have anything suitable. We are both totally incompetent to decide on such a delicate matter, but we will trust entirely to your judgment in the selection.' The milliner was quite collected by this time, as she asked, 'Any particular style?—and about what price?'

" 'The price is immaterial,' said he disdainfully. 'Any man who will wager on the average weight of a trainload of cattle, his own cattle, mind you, and miss them twenty pounds, ought to pay for his lack of judgment. Don't you think so, Miss—er—er? Excuse me for being unable to call your name—but—but—'

" 'De Ment is my name,' said she with some little embarrassment.

" 'Livingstone is mine,' said he with a profound bow, 'and this gentleman is Mr. Ochiltree, youngest brother of Congressman Tom. Now regarding the style, we will depend entirely upon your selection. But possibly the loser is entitled to some choice in the matter. Mr. Ochiltree, have you any preference in regard to style?'

" 'Why, no, I can generally tell whether a hat becomes a lady or not, but as to selecting one I am at sea. We had better depend on Miss De Ment's judgment. Still, I always like an abundance of flowers on a lady's hat. Whenever a girl walks down the street ahead of me, I like to watch the posies, grass, and buds on her hat wave and nod with the motion of her walk. Miss De Ment, don't you agree with me that an abundance of flowers becomes a young lady? And this girl can't be over twenty.'

" 'Well, now,' said she, going into matters in earnest, 'I can scarcely advise you. Is the young lady a brunette or blonde?'

" 'What difference does that make?' he innocently asked.

" 'Oh,' said she, smiling, 'we must harmonize colors. What would suit one complexion would not become another. What color is her hair?'

" 'Nearly the color of yours,' said he. 'Not so heavy and lacks the natural wave which yours has—but she's all right. She can ride a string of my horses until they all have sore backs. I tell you she is a cute trick. But, say, Miss De Ment, what do you think of a green hat, broad-brimmed, turned up behind and on one side, long black feathers run round and turned up behind, with a blue bird on the other side swooping down like a pigeon hawk, long tail feathers and an arrow in its beak? That strikes me as about the mustard. What do you think of that kind of hat, dear?'

" 'Why, sir, the colors don't harmonize,' she replied, blushing.

" 'Theodore, do you know anything about this harmony of colors? Excuse me, madam—and I crave your pardon, Mr. Ochiltree, for using your given name—but really this harmony of colors is all French to me.'

" 'Well, if the young lady is in town, why can't you have her drop in and make her own selection?' suggested the blond milliner.

"He studied a moment, and then awoke as if from a trance. 'Just as easy as not; this very evening or in the morning. Strange we didn't think of that sooner. Yes, the landlady of the hotel can join us, and we can count on your assistance in selecting the hat.' With a number of comments on her attractive place, inquiries regarding trade, and a flattering compliment on having made such a charming acquaintance, we edged towards the door. 'This evening, then, or in the morning at the farthest, you may expect another call, when my friend must pay the penalty of his folly by settling the bill. Put it on heavy.' And he gave her a parting wink.

"Together we bowed ourselves out, and once safe in the street he said, 'Didn't she help us out of that easy? If she wasn't a blonde, I'd go back and buy her two hats for suggesting it as she did.'

" 'Rather good-looking too,' I remarked.

" 'Oh, well, that's a matter of taste. I like people with red blood in them. Now if you was to saw her arm off, it wouldn't bleed; just a little white water might ooze out, possibly. The best-looking girl I ever saw was down in the lower Rio Grande country, and she was milking a goat. Theodore, my dear fellow, when I'm led blushingly to the altar, you'll be proud of my choice. I'm a judge of beauty.' "

It was after midnight when we disposed of the first oven of pigeon potpie, and, wrapping ourselves in blankets, lay down around the fire. With the first sign of dawn, we were aroused by Mr. Nathan and Uncle Lance to witness the return flight of the birds to their feeding grounds. Hurrying to the nearest opening, we saw the immense flight of pigeons blackening the sky overhead. Stiffened by their night's rest, they flew low; but the beauty and immensity of the flight overawed us, and we stood in mute admiration, no one firing a shot. For fully a half hour the flight continued, ending in a few scattering birds.

I'd Have Gambled My Life on Her

told by
Add Tully

When we reached the camp shortly before dark, we found the others had already arrived, ours making the sixth turkey in the evening's bag. We had drawn ours on killing it, as had the others, and after supper Uncle Lance superintended the stuffing of the two largest birds. While this was in progress, others made a stiff mortar, and we coated each turkey with about three inches of the waxy clay, feathers and all. Opening our campfire, we placed the turkeys together, covered them with ashes and built a heaping fire over and around them. A number of haunts had been located by the others, but as we expected to make an early hunt in the morning, we decided not to visit any of the roosts that night. After Uncle Lance had regaled us with hunting stories of an early day, the discussion innocently turned to my recent unsuccessful elopement. By this time the scars had healed fairly well, and I took the chaffing in all good humor. Tully told a personal experience, which, if it was the truth, argued that in time I might become as indifferent to my recent mishap as anyone could wish.

"My prospects of marrying a few years ago," said Tully, lying full stretch before the fire, "were a whole lot better than yours, Quirk. But my ambition those days was to boss a herd up the trail and get topnotch wages. She was a Texas girl, just like yours, bred up in Van Zandt County. She could ride a horse like an Indian. Bad horses seemed afraid of her. Why, I saw her once when she was about sixteen, take a black stallion out of his stable, lead him out with but a rope about his neck, throw a half hitch about his nose, and mount him as though he was her pet. Bareback and without a bridle she rode him ten miles for a doctor. There wasn't a mile of the distance either but he felt the quirt burning in his flank and knew he was being ridden by a master. Her father scolded her at the time, and boasted about it later.

"She had dozens of admirers, and the first impression I ever made on her was when she was about twenty.

There was a big tournament being given, and all the young bloods in many counties came in to contest for the prizes. I was a double winner in the games and contests—won a roping prize and was the only lad that came inside the time limit as a lancer, though several beat me on rings. Of course, the tournament ended with a ball. Having won the lance prize, it was my privilege of crowning the 'queen' of the ball. Of course, I wasn't going to throw away such a chance, for there was no end of rivalry amongst the girls over it. The crown was made of flowers, or if there were none in season, of live-oak leaves. Well, at the ball after the tournament I crowned Miss Kate with a crown of oak leaves. After that I felt bold enough to crowd matters, and things came my way. We were to be married during Easter week, but her mother up and died, so we put it off awhile for the sake of appearances.

"The next spring I got a chance to boss a herd up the trail for Jesse Ellison. It was the chance of my life and I couldn't think of refusing. The girl put up quite a mouth about it, and I explained to her that a hundred a month wasn't offered to every man. She finally gave in, but still you could see she wasn't pleased. Girls that way don't sabe cattle matters a little bit. She promised to write me at several points which I told her the herd would pass. When I bade her good-by, tears stood in her eyes, though she tried to hide them. I'd have gambled my life on her that morning.

"Well, we had a nice trip, good outfit and strong cattle. Uncle Jesse mounted us ten horses to the man, every one fourteen hands or better, for we were contracted for delivery in Nebraska. It was a five months' drive with scarcely an incident on the way. Just a run or two and a dry drive or so. I had lots of time to think about Kate. When we reached the Chisholm crossing on Red River, I felt certain that I would find a letter, but I didn't. I wrote her from there, but when we reached Caldwell, nary a letter either. The same luck at Abilene. Try as I might, I couldn't make it out. Something was wrong, but what it was, was anybody's guess.

"At this last place we got our orders to deliver the cattle at the junction of the middle and lower Loup. It was a terror of a long drive, but that wasn't a circumstance compared to not hearing from Kate. I kept all this to myself, mind you. When our herd reached its destination, which it did on time, as hard luck would have it there was a hitch in the payment. The herd was turned loose and all the outfit but myself sent home. I stayed there two months longer at a little place called Broken Bow. I held the bill of sale for the herd, and would turn it over, transferring the cattle from one owner to another, on the word from my employer. At last I received a letter from Uncle Jesse saying that the payment in full had been made, so I surrendered the final document and came home. Those trains seemed to run awful slow. But I got home all too soon, for she had then been married three months.

"You see, an agent for eight-day clocks came along, and being a stranger took her eye. He was one of those nice, dapper fellows, wore a red necktie, and could talk all day to a woman. He worked by the rule of three—tickle, talk, and flatter, with a few cutes thrown in for a pilon; that gets nearly any of them. They live in town now. He's a windmill agent. I never went near them."

Meanwhile the fire kept pace with the talk, thanks to Uncle Lance's watchful eye. "That's right, Tiburcio, carry up plenty of good *leña,*" he kept saying. "Bring in all the blackjack oak that you can find; it makes fine coals. These are both big gobblers, and to bake them until they fall to pieces like a watermelon will require a steady fire till morning. Pile up a lot of wood, and if I wake up during the night, trust to me to look after the fire. I've baked so many turkeys this way that I'm an expert at the business."

Miss Sallie of Shot-a-Buck Crossing

told by
June Deweese

At the next pause in the yarning, I inquired why a wild turkey always deceived itself by hiding its head and leaving the body exposed. "That it's a fact, we all know," volunteered Uncle Lance, "but the why and wherefore is too deep for me. I take it that it's due to running to neck too much in their construction. Now an ostrich is the same way, all neck with not a lick of sense. And the same applies to the human family. You take one of these long-necked cowmen and what does he know outside of cattle? Nine times out of ten, I can tell a sensible girl by merely looking at her neck. Now snicker, you dratted young fools, just as if I wasn't talking horse sense to you. Some of you boys haven't got much more sabe than a fat old gobbler."

"When I first came to this state," said June Deweese, who had been quietly and attentively listening to the stories, "I stopped over on the Neches River near a place called Shot-a-Buck Crossing. I had an uncle living there with whom I made my home the first few years that I lived in Texas. There are more or less cattle there, but it is principally a cotton country. There was an old cuss living over there on that river who was land poor, but had a powerful purty girl. Her old man owned any number of plantations on the river—generally had lots of nigger renters to look after. Miss Sallie, the daughter, was the belle of the neighborhood. She had all the graces with a fair mixture of the weaknesses of her sex. The trouble was, there was no young man in the whole country fit to hold her horse. At least she and her folks entertained that idea. There was a storekeeper and a young doctor at the county seat, who it seems took turns calling on her. It looked like it was going to be a close race. Outside of these two there wasn't one of us who could touch her with a twenty-four-foot fish-pole. We simply took the side of the road when she passed by.

"About this time there drifted in from out west near

Fort McKavett, a young fellow named Curly Thorn. He had relatives living in that neighborhood. Out at the fort he was a common foreman on a ranch. Talk about your graceful riders, he sat a horse in a manner that left nothing to be desired. Well, Curly made himself very agreeable with all the girls on the range, but played no special favorites. He stayed in the country, visiting among cousins, until camp meeting began over at the Alabama Camp Ground. During this meeting Curly proved himself quite a gallant by carrying first one young lady and the next evening some other to camp meeting. During these two weeks of the meeting, someone introduced him to Miss Sallie. Now, remember, he didn't play her for a favorite no more than any other. That's what miffed her. She thought he ought to.

"One Sunday afternoon she intimated to him, like a girl sometimes will, that she was going home, and was sorry that she had no companion for the ride. This was sufficient for the gallant Curly to offer himself to her as an escort. She simply thought she was stealing a beau from some other girl, and he never dreamt he was dallying with Neches River royalty. But the only inequality in that couple as they rode away from the ground was an erroneous idea in her and her folks' minds. And that difference was in the fact that her old dad had more land than he could pay taxes on. Well, Curly not only saw her home, but stayed for tea—that's the name the girls have for supper over on the Neches—and that night carried her back to the evening service. From that day till the close of the session he was devotedly hers. A month afterward when he left, it was the talk of the country that they were to be married during the coming holidays.

"But then there were the young doctor and the storekeeper still in the game. Curly was off the scene temporarily, but the other two were riding their best horses to a shadow. Miss Sallie's folks were pulling like bay steers for the merchant, who had some money, while the young doctor had nothing but empty pill bags and a saddle horse or two. The doctor was the better looking, and, before meeting Curly Thorn, Miss Sallie had favored him. Knowing ones said they were engaged. But near the close of the race there was sufficient home influence used for the storekeeper to take the lead and hold it until the showdown came. Her folks announced the wedding, and the merchant received the best wishes of his friends, while the young doctor took a trip for his health. Well, it developed afterwards that she was engaged to both the storekeeper and the doctor at the same time. But that's nothing. My experience tells me that a girl don't need broad shoulders to carry three or four engagements at the same time.

"Well, within a week of the wedding, who should drift in to spend Christmas but Curly Thorn. His cousins, of course, lost no time in giving him the lay of the land. But Curly acted indifferent, and never even offered to call on Miss Sallie. Us fellows joked him about his girl going to marry another fellow, and he didn't seem a little bit put out. In fact, he seemed to enjoy the sudden turn as a good joke on himself. But one morning, two days before the wedding was to take place, Miss Sallie was missing from her home, as was likewise Curly

Thorn from the neighborhood. Yes, Thorn had eloped with her and they were married the next morning in Nacogdoches. And the funny thing about it was, Curly never met her after his return until the night they eloped. But he had a girl cousin who had a finger in the pie. She and Miss Sallie were as thick as three in a bed, and Curly didn't have anything to do but play the hand that was dealt him.

"Before I came to Las Palomas, I was over round Fort McKavett and met Curly. We knew each other, and he took me home and had me stay overnight with him. They had been married then four years. She had a baby on each knee and another in her arms. There was so much reality in life that she had no time to become a dreamer. Matrimony in that case was a good leveler of imaginary rank. I always admired Curly for the indifferent hand he played all through the various stages of the courtship. He never knew there was such a thing as difference. He simply coppered the play to win, and the cards came his way."

"Bully for Curly!" said Uncle Lance, arising and fixing the fire, as the rest of us unrolled our blankets. "If some of my rascals could make a ten strike like that it would break a streak of bad luck which has overshadowed Las Palomas for over thirty years. Great Scott!—but those gobblers smell good. I can hear them blubbering and sizzling in their shells. It will surely take an axe to crack that clay in the morning. But get under your blankets, lads, for I'll call you for a turkey breakfast about dawn."

Scared Horses on the Navidad

told by
Aaron Scales

We made camp early that evening on the home river, opposite the range of the *manada*. Sending out Pasquale to locate the band and watch them until dark, Uncle Lance outlined his idea of circling the band and bagging the outlaw in the uncertain light of dawn. Pasquale reported on his return after dark that the *manada* were contentedly feeding on their accustomed range within three miles of camp. Pasquale had watched the band for an hour, and described the *ladino* stallion as a cinnamon-colored coyote, splendidly proportioned and unusually large for a mustang.

Naturally, in expectation of the coming sport, the horses became the topic around the campfire that night. Every man present was a born horseman, and there was a generous rivalry for the honor in telling horse stories. Aaron Scales joined the group at a fortunate time to introduce an incident from his own experience, and, raking out a coal of fire for his pipe, began:

"The first ranch I ever worked on," said he, "was located on the Navidad in Lavaca County. It was quite a new country then, rather broken and timbered in places and full of bear and wolves. Our outfit was working some cattle before the general roundup in the spring. We wanted to move one brand to another range as soon as the grass would permit, and we were gathering them for that purpose. We had some ninety saddle horses with us to do the work—sufficient to mount fifteen men.

"One night we camped in a favorite spot, and as we had no cattle to hold that night, all the horses were thrown loose, with the usual precaution of hobbling, except two or three on picket. All but about ten head wore the bracelets, and those ten were pals, their pardners wearing the hemp. Early in the evening, probably nine o'clock, with a bright fire burning, and the boys spreading down their beds for the night, suddenly the horses were heard running, and the next moment they hobbled into camp like a school of porpoise, trampling over the beds and crowding up to the fire and the wagon. They almost knocked down some of the boys, so sudden was their entrance. Then they set up a terrible nickering for mates. The boys went amongst them, and horses that were timid and shy almost caressed their riders, trembling in limb and muscle the while through fear, like a leaf.

"We concluded a bear had scented the camp, and in approaching it had circled round, and run amuck our saddle horses. Every horse by instinct is afraid of a bear, but more particularly a range-raised one. It's the same instinct that makes it impossible to ride or drive a range-raised horse over a rattlesnake.

"Well, after the boys had petted their mounts and quieted their fears, they were still reluctant to leave camp, but stood around for several hours, evidently feeling more secure in our presence. Now and then one of the free ones would graze out a little distance, cautiously sniff the air, then trot back to the others. We built up a big fire to scare away any bear or wolves that might be in the vicinity, but the horses stayed like invited guests, perfectly contented as long as we would pet them and talk to them. Some of the boys crawled under the wagon, hoping to get a little sleep, rather than spread their bed where a horse could stampede over it.

"Near midnight we took ropes and saddle blankets and drove them several hundred yards from camp. The rest of the night we slept with one eye open, expecting every moment to hear them take fright and return. They didn't, but at daylight every horse was within five hundred yards of the wagon, and when we unhobbled them and broke camp that morning, we had to throw riders in the lead to hold them back."

A Drive from the San Saba to the Concho

told by
Theodore Quayle

On the conclusion of Scales's experience, there was no lack of volunteers to take up the thread, though an unwritten law forbade interruptions. Our employer was among the group, and out of deference to our guest, Captain Frank Byler, the boys remained silent. Uncle Lance finally regaled us with an account of a fight between range stallions which he had once witnessed, and on its conclusion Theodore Quayle took his turn.

"The man I was working for once moved nearly a thousand head of mixed range stock, of which about three hundred were young mules, from the San Saba to the Concho River. It was a dry country and we were compelled to follow the McKavett and Fort Chadbourne trail. We had timed our drives so that we reached creeks once a day at least, sometimes oftener. It was the latter part of summer, and was unusually hot and drouthy. There was one drive of twenty-five miles ahead that the owner knew of without water, and we had planned this drive so as to reach it at noon, drive halfway, make a dry camp overnight, and reach the pools by noon the next day. Imagine our chagrin on reaching the watering place to find the stream dry. We lost several hours riding up and down the arroyo in the hope of finding relief for the men, if not for the stock. It had been dusty for weeks. The cook had a little water in his keg, but only enough for drinking purposes. It was twenty miles yet to the Concho, and make it before night we must. Turning back was farther than going ahead, and the afternoon was fearfully hot. The heat waves looked like a sea of fire. The first part of the afternoon drive was a gradual ascent for fifteen miles, and then came a narrow plateau of a divide. As we reached this mesa, a sorrier-looking lot of men, horses, and mules can hardly be imagined. We had already traveled over forty miles without water for the stock, and five more lay between us and the coveted river.

"The heat was oppressive to the men, but the herd suffered most from the fine alkali dust which enveloped them. Their eyebrows and nostrils were whitened with this fine powder, while all colors merged into one. On reaching this divide, we could see the cottonwoods that outlined the stream ahead. Before we had fully crossed this watershed and begun the descent, the mules would trot along beside the riders in the lead, even permitting us to lay our hands on their backs. It was getting late in the day before the first friendly breeze of the afternoon blew softly in our faces. Then, great Scott! what a change came over man and herd. The mules in front threw up their heads and broke into a grand chorus. Those that were strung out took up the refrain and trotted forward. The horses set up a rival concert in a higher key. They had scented the water five miles off.

"All hands except one man on each side now rode in the lead. Every once in a while, some enthusiastic mule would break through the line of horsemen, and would have to be brought back. Every time we came to an elevation where we could catch the breeze, the grand horse-and-mule concert would break out anew. At the last elevation between us and the water, several mules broke through, and before they could be brought back the whole herd had broken into a run which was impossible to check. We opened out then and let them go.

"The Concho was barely running, but had long, deep pools here and there, into which horses and mules plunged, dropped down, rolled over, and then got up to nicker and bray. The young mules did everything but drink, while the horses were crazy with delight. When the wagon came up we went into camp and left them to play out their hands. There was no herding to do that night, as the water would hold them as readily as a hundred men."

"Well, I'm going to hunt my blankets," said Uncle Lance, rising. "You understand, Captain Byler, that you are to sleep with me tonight. Davy Crockett once said that the politest man he ever met in Washington simply set out the decanter and glasses, and then walked over and looked out of the window while he took a drink. Now I want to be equally polite and don't want to hurry you to sleep, but whenever you get tired of yarning, you'll find the bed with me in it to the windward of that live-oak tree top over yonder."

Captain Frank showed no inclination to accept the invitation just then, but assured his host that he would join him later.

Chasing Mustangs

told by
Dan Happersett

After Uncle Lance had sought his blankets, an hour or two passed by while the yarning continued.

"Haven't you fellows gone to bed yet?" came an inquiry from out of a fallen tree top beyond the fire in a voice which we all recognized. "All right, boys, sit up all night and tell fool stories if you want to. But remember, I'll have the last rascal of you in the saddle an hour before daybreak. I have little sympathy for a man who won't sleep when he has a good chance. So if you don't turn in at all it will be all right, but you'll be routed out at three in the morning, and the man who requires a second calling will get a bucket of water in his face."

Captain Frank and several of us rose expecting to take the hint of our employer, when our good intentions were arrested by a query from Dan Happersett, "Did any of you ever walk down a wild horse?" None of us had, and we turned back and reseated ourselves in the group.

"I had a little whirl of it once when I was a youngster," said Dan, "except we didn't walk. It was well known that there were several bands of wild horses ranging in the southwest corner of Tom Green County. Those who had seen them described one band as numbering forty to fifty head with a fine chestnut stallion as a leader. Their range was well located when water was plentiful, but during certain months of the year the shallow lagoons where they watered dried up, and they were compelled to leave. It was when they were forced to go to other waters that glimpses of them were to be had, and then only at a distance of one or two miles. There was an outfit made up one spring to go out to their range and walk these horses down. This season of the year was selected, as the lagoons would be full of water and the horses would be naturally reduced in flesh and strength after the winter, as well as weak and thin-blooded from their first taste of grass. We took along two wagons, one loaded with grain for our mounts.

These saddle horses had been eating grain for months before we started and their flesh was firm and solid.

"We headed for the lagoons, which were known to a few of our party, and when we came within ten miles of the water holes, we saw fresh signs of a band—places where they had apparently grazed within a week. But it was the second day before we caught sight of the wild horses, and too late in the day to give them chase. They were watering at a large lake south of our camp, and we did not disturb them. We watched them until nightfall, and that night we planned to give them chase at daybreak. Four of us were to do the riding by turns, and imaginary stations were allotted to the four quarters of our camp. If they refused to leave their range and circled, we could send them at least a hundred and fifty miles the first day, ourselves riding possibly a hundred, and this riding would be divided among four horses, with plenty of fresh ones at camp for a change.

"Being the lightest rider in the party, it was decided that I was to give them the first chase. We had a crafty plainsman for our captain, and long before daylight he and I rode out and waited for the first peep of day. Before the sun had risen, we sighted the wild herd within a mile of the place where darkness had settled over them the night previous. With a few parting instructions from our captain, I rode leisurely between them and the lake where they had watered the evening before. At first sight of me they took fright and ran to a slight elevation. There they halted a moment, craning their necks and sniffing the air. This was my first fair view of the chestnut stallion. He refused to break into a gallop, and even stopped before the rest, turning defiantly on this intruder of his domain. From the course I was riding, every moment I was expecting them to catch the wind of me. Suddenly they scented me, knew me for an enemy, and with the stallion in the lead they were off to the south.

"It was an exciting ride that morning. Without a halt they ran twenty miles to the south, then turned to the left and there halted on an elevation; but a shot in the air told them that all was not well and they moved on. For an hour and a half they kept their course to the east, and at last turned to the north. This was, as we had calculated, about their range. In another hour at the farthest, a new rider with a fresh horse would take up the running. My horse was still fresh and enjoying the chase, when on a swell of the plain I made out the rider who was to relieve me; and though it was early yet in the day the mustangs had covered sixty miles to my forty. When I saw my relief locate the band, I turned and rode leisurely to camp. When the last two riders came into camp that night, they reported having left the herd at a new lake, to which the mustang had led them, some fifteen miles from our camp to the westward.

"Each day for the following week was a repetition of the first with varying incident. But each day it was plain to be seen that they were fagging fast. Toward the evening of the eighth day, the rider dared not crowd them for fear of their splitting into small bands, a thing to be avoided. On the ninth day two riders took them at a time, pushing them unmercifully but preventing them from splitting, and in the evening of this day they could be turned at the will of the riders. It was then agreed that after a half day's chase on the morrow, they could be handled with ease. By noon next day, we had driven them within a mile of our camp.

"They were tired out and we turned them into an impromptu corral made of wagons and ropes. All but the chestnut stallion. At the last he escaped us; he stopped on a little knoll and took a farewell look at his band.

"There were four old United States cavalry horses among our captive band of mustangs, gray with age and worthless—no telling where they came from. We clamped a muleshoe over the pasterns of the younger horses, tied toggles to the others, and the next morning set out on our return to the settlements."

Under his promise the old ranchero had the camp astir over an hour before dawn.

Indian-Style Fun

told by
Vick Wolf

The cook was ordered to set out the best the wagon afforded, several outside delicacies were added, and a feast was in sight. Gee Gee Cederdall had recrossed the river that day to mail a letter, and on his return proudly carried a basket of eggs on his arm. Three of the others had joined a seining party from the Texas side, and had come in earlier in the day with a fine string of fish. Parent won new laurels in the supper to which he invited us about sundown. The cattle came in to their beds groaning and satiated, and dropped down as if ordered. When the first watch had taken them, there was nothing to do but sit around and tell stories. Since crossing Red River, we had slept almost night and day, but in that balmy May evening sleep was banished. The fact that we were in the Indian country, civilized though the Indians were, called forth many an incident. The raids of the Comanches into the Panhandle country during the buffalo days was a favorite topic. Vick Wolf, however, had had an Indian experience in the North with which he regaled us at the first opportunity.

"There isn't any trouble nowadays," said he, lighting a cigarette, "with these blanket Indians on the reservations. I had an experience once on a reservation where the Indians could have got me easy enough if they had been on the warpath. It was the first winter I ever spent on a Northern range, having gone up to the Cherokee Strip to avoid—well, no matter. I got a job in the Strip, not riding, but as a kind of an all-round rustler. This was long before the country was fenced, and they rode lines to keep the cattle on their ranges. One evening about nightfall in December, the worst kind of a blizzard struck us that the country had ever seen. The next day it was just as bad, and *bloody* cold. A fellow could not see any distance, and to venture away from the dugout meant to get lost. The third day she broke and the sun came out clear in the early evening.

The next day we managed to gather the saddle horses, as they had not drifted like the cattle.

"Well, we were three days overtaking the lead of that cattle drift, and then found them in the heart of the Cheyenne country, at least on that reservation. They had drifted a good hundred miles before the storm broke. Every outfit in the Strip had gone south after their cattle. Instead of drifting them back together, the different ranches rustled for their own. Some of the foremen paid the Indians so much per head to gather for them, but ours didn't. The braves weren't very much struck on us on that account. I was cooking for the outfit, which suited me in winter weather. We had a permanent camp on a small well-wooded creek, from which we worked all the country round.

"One afternoon when I was in camp all alone, I noticed an Indian approaching me from out of the timber. There was a Winchester standing against the wagon wheel, but as the bucks were making no trouble, I gave the matter no attention. Mr. Injun came up to the fire and professed to be very friendly, shook hands, and spoke quite a number of words in English. After he got good and warm, he looked all over the wagon, and noticing that I had no six-shooter on, he picked up the carbine and walked out about a hundred yards to a little knoll, threw his arms in the air, and made signs.

"Instantly, out of the cover of some timber on the creek a quarter mile above, came about twenty young bucks, mounted, and yelling like demons. When they came up, they began circling around the fire and wagon. I was sitting on an empty corn crate by the fire. One young buck, seeing that I was not scaring to suit him, unslung a carbine as he rode, and shot into the fire before me. The bullet threw fire and ashes all over me, and I jumped about ten feet, which suited them better. They circled around for several minutes, every one uncovering a carbine, and they must have fired a hundred and fifty shots into the fire. In fact, they almost shot it out, scattering the fire around so that it came near burning up the bedding of our outfit. I was scared thoroughly by this time. If it was possible for me to have had fits, I'd have had one sure. The air seemed full of coals of fire and ashes. I got good practical insight into what hell's like. I was rustling the rolls of bedding out of the circle of fire, expecting every moment would be my last. It's a wonder I wasn't killed. Were they throwing lead? Well, I should remark! You see, the ground was not frozen around the fire, and the bullets buried themselves in the soft soil.

"After they had had as much fun as they wanted, the leader gave a yell and they all circled the other way once, and struck back into the timber. Some of them had brought up the decoy Indian's horse when they made the dash at first, and he suddenly turned as wild as a Cheyenne generally gets. When the others were several hundred yards away, he turned his horse, rode back some little distance, and attracted my attention by holding out the Winchester. From his horse he laid it carefully down on the ground, whirled his pony, and rode like a scared wolf after the others. I could hear their yells for miles, as they made for their encampment over on the North Fork. As soon as I got the fire under control, I went out and got the carbine. It was empty; the Indian had used its magazine in the general hilarity. That may be an Indian's style of fun, but I failed to see where there was any in it for me."

The cook threw a handful of oily fish bones on the fire, causing it to flame up for a brief moment. With the exception of Wayne Outcault, who was lying prone on the ground, the men were smoking and sitting Indian fashion around the fire. After rolling awhile uneasily, Outcault sat up and remarked, "I feel about half sick. Eat too much? Don't you think it. Why, I only ate seven or eight of those fish, and that oughtn't to hurt a baby. There was only half a dozen hard-boiled eggs to the man, and I don't remember of any of you being so generous as to share yours with me. Those few plates of prunes that I ate for dessert wouldn't hurt nobody—they're medicine to some folks. Unroll our bed, pardner, and I'll thrash around on it awhile."

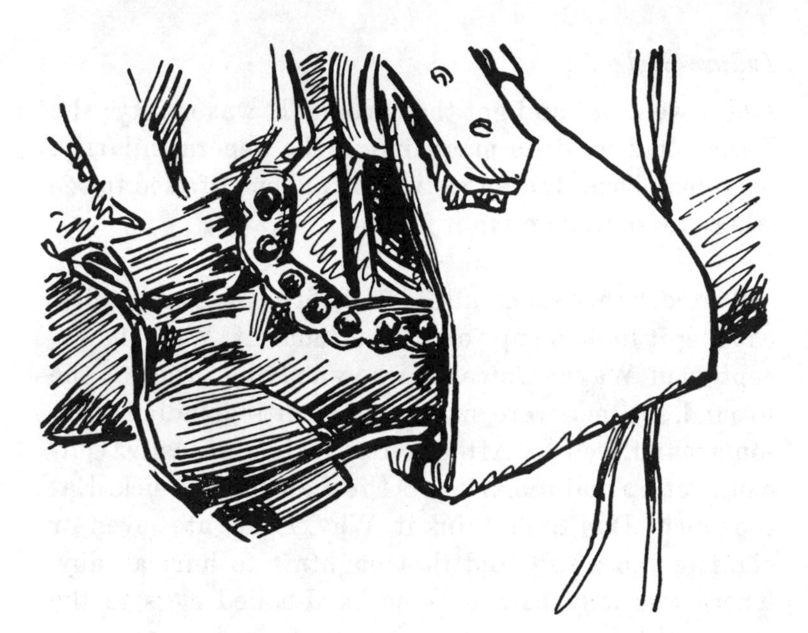

Button Shoes and the Big Auger

told by
Runt Pickett

Several trail stories of more or less interest had been told, when Runt Pickett, in order to avoid the smoke, came over and sat down between Burl Van Vedder and me. He had had an experience, and instantly opened on us at short range.

"Speaking of stampedes," said Runt, "reminds me

of a run I was in, and over which I was paid by my employer a very high compliment. My first trip over the trail, as far north as Dodge, was in '78. The herd sold next day after reaching there, and as I had an old uncle and aunt living in middle Kansas, I concluded to run down and pay them a short visit. So I threw away all my trail togs—well, they were worn out, anyway—and bought me a new outfit complete. Yes, I even bought button shoes. After visiting a couple of weeks with my folks, I drifted back to Dodge in the hope of getting in with some herd bound farther north—I was perfectly useless on a farm. On my return to Dodge, the only thing about me that indicated a cowhand was my Texas saddle and outfit, but in toggery, in my visiting harness, I looked like a rank tenderfoot.

"Well, boys, the first day I struck town I met a through man looking for hands. His herd had just come in over the Chisholm Trail, crossing to the Western somewhere above. He was disgusted with his outfit, and was discharging men right and left and hiring new ones to take their places. I apologized for my appearance, showed him my outfit, and got a job cowpunching with this through man. He expected to hold on sale a week or two, when if unsold he would drift north to the Platte. The first week that I worked, a wet stormy night struck us, and before ten o'clock we lost every hoof of cattle. I was riding wild after little squads of cattle here and there, guided by flashes of lightning, when the storm finally broke. Well, there it was midnight, and I didn't have a *hoof of cattle* to hold and no one to help me if I had. The truth is, I was lost. Common horse sense told me that; but where the outfit or wagon was was anybody's guess. The horses in my mount were as good as worthless; worn out, and if you gave one free rein he lacked the energy to carry you back to camp. I ploughed around in the darkness for over an hour, but finally came to a sudden stop on the banks of the muddy Arkansas. Right there I held a council of war with myself, the decision of which was that it was at least five miles to the wagon.

"After I'd prowled around some little time, a bright flash of lightning revealed to me an old deserted cabin a few rods below. To this shelter I turned without even a bid, unsaddled my horse and picketed him, and turned into the cabin for the night. Early the next morning I was out and saddled my horse, and the question was, which way is camp? As soon as the sun rose clearly, I got my bearings. By my reasoning, if the river yesterday was south of camp, this morning the wagon must be north of the river, so I headed in that direction. Somehow or other I stopped my horse on the first little knoll, and looking back towards the bottom, I saw in a horseshoe which the river made a large bunch of cattle. Of course, I knew that all herds near about were through cattle and under herd, and the absence of any men in sight aroused my curiosity. I concluded to investigate it, and riding back found over five hundred head of the cattle we had lost the night before. 'Here's a chance to make a record with my new boss,' I said to myself, and circling in behind, began drifting them out of the bottoms towards the uplands. By ten o'clock I had got them to the first divide, when who should ride up but the owner, the old cowman himself—the sure enough big auger.

" 'Well, son,' said my boss, 'you held some of them, didn't you?'

" 'Yes,' I replied, surly as I could, giving him a mean look, 'I've nearly ridden this horse to death, holding this bunch all night. If I had only had a good man or two with me, we could have caught twice as many. What kind of an outfit are you working, anyhow, Captain?'

"And at dinner that day, the boss pointed me out to the others and said, 'That little fellow standing over there with the button shoes on is the only man in my outfit that is worth a —— ——.' "

Bogged to the Saddle Skirts in the Story

told by
John Levering

The cook had finished his work, and now joined the circle. Parent began regaling us with personal experiences, in which it was evident that he would prove the hero. Fortunately, however, we were spared listening to his self-laudation. Dorg Seay and Tim Stanley, bunkies, engaged in a friendly scuffle, each trying to make the other get a firebrand for his pipe. In the tussle which followed, we were all compelled to give way or get trampled underfoot. When both had exhausted themselves in vain, we resumed our places around the fire. Parent, who was disgusted over the interruption, on resuming his seat refused to continue his story at the request of the offenders, replying, "The more I see of you two varmints the more you remind me of mule colts."

Once the cook refused to pick up the broken thread of his story, John Levering, our horse wrangler, preempted the vacated post.

"I was over in Louisiana a few winters ago with a horse herd," said John, "and had a few experiences. Of all the simple people that I ever met, the 'Cajin' takes the bakery. You'll meet darkies over there that can't speak a word of anything but French. It's nothing to see a cow and mule harnessed together to a cart. One day on the road, I met a man, old enough to be my father, and inquired of him how far it was to the parish center, a large town. He didn't know, except it was a long, long ways. He had never been there, but his older brother, once when he was a young man, had been there as a witness at court. The brother was dead now, but if he was living and present, it was quite possible that he would remember the distance. The best information was that it was a very long ways off. I rode it in the mud in less than two hours; just about ten miles.

"But that wasn't a circumstance to other experiences. We had driven about three hundred horses and mules, and after disposing of over two thirds of them, my employer was compelled to return home, leaving me to dispose of the remainder. I was a fair salesman, and rather than carry the remnant of the herd with me, made headquarters with a man who owned a large canebrake pasture. It was a convenient stopping place, and the stock did well on the young cane. Every week I would drive to some distant town eighteen or twenty head, or as many as I could handle alone. Sometimes I would sell out in a few days, and then again it would take me longer. But when possible I always made it a rule to get back to my headquarters to spend Sunday. The owner of the canebrake and his wife were a simple couple, and just a shade or two above the Arcadians. But they had a daughter who could pass muster, and she took quite a shine to the Texas-Hoss-Man, as they called me. I reckon you understand now why I made that headquarters?—there were other reasons besides the good pasturage.

"Well, the girl and her mother both could read, but I have some doubt about the old man on that score. They took no papers, and the nearest approach to a book in the house was an almanac three years old. The women folks were ravenous for something to read, and each time on my return after selling out, I'd bring them a whole bundle of illustrated papers and magazines. About my fourth return after more horses—I was mighty near one of the family by that time—when we were all seated around the fire one night, the women poring over the papers and admiring the pictures, the old man inquired what the news was over in the parish where I had recently been. The only thing that I could remember was the suicide of a prominent man. After explaining the circumstances, I went on to say that some little bitterness arose over his burial. Owing to his prominence it was thought permission would be given to bury him in the churchyard. But it seems there was some superstition about permitting a self-murderer to be buried in the same field as decent folks. It was none of my funeral, and I didn't pay overmuch attention to the matter, but the authorities refused, and they buried him just outside the grounds, in the woods.

"My host and I discussed the matter at some length. He contended that if the man was not of sound mind, he should have been given his little six feet of earth among the others. A horse salesman has to be a good second-rate talker, and being anxious to show off before the girl, I differed with her father. The argument grew spirited yet friendly, and I appealed to the women in supporting my view. My hostess was absorbed at the time in reading a sensational account of a woman shooting her betrayer. The illustrations covered a whole page, and the girl was simply burning, at short range, the shirt from off her seducer. The old lady was bogged to the saddle skirts in the story, when I interrupted her and inquired, 'Mother, what do you think ought to be done with a man who commits suicide?'

"She lowered the paper just for an instant, and looking over her spectacles at me replied, 'Well, I think any man who would do *that* ought to be made to support the child.' "

Pig-Fat and Slick as Weasels

told by
Paul Priest

What an evening and night that was! As we passed up the creek, we sighted in the gathering twilight the campfires of Sponsilier and my brother, several miles apart and south of the stream. When we reached Forrest's wagon the clans were gathering, Paul Priest—the Rebel—and his crowd being the last to come in from above. Groups of saddle horses were tied among the trees, while around two fires were circles of men broiling beef over live coals. The red-headed cook had anticipated forty guests outside of his own outfit, and was pouring coffee into tin cups and shying biscuit right and left on request. The supper was a success, not on account of the spread or our superior table manners, but we graced the occasion with appetites which required the staples of life to satisfy. Then we smoked, falling into groups when the yarning began. All the fresh-beef stories of our lives, and they were legion, were told, no one group paying any attention to another.

"Every time I run afoul of fresh beef," said the Rebel, as he settled back comfortably between the roots of a cottonwood, with his back to its trunk, "it reminds me of the time I was a prisoner among the Yankees. It was the last year of the war, and I had got over my first desire to personally whip the whole North. There were about five thousand of us held as prisoners of war for eleven months on a peninsula in the Chesapeake Bay. The fighting spirit of the soldier was broken in the majority of us, especially among the older men and those who had families. But we youngsters accepted the fortunes of war and were glad that we were alive, even if we were prisoners. In my mess in prison there were fifteen, all having been captured at the same time, and many of us comrades of three years' standing.

"I remember the day we were taken off the train and marched through the town for the prison, a Yankee band in our front playing national airs and favorites of their army, and the people along the route jeering us and asking how we liked the music. Our mess held together during the march, and some of the boys answered them back as well as they could. Once inside the prison stockade, we went into quarters and our mess still held together. Before we had been there long, one day there was a call among the prisoners for volunteers to form a roustabout crew. Well, I enlisted as a roustabout. We had to report to an officer twice a day, and then were put under guard and set to work. The kind of labor I liked best was unloading the supplies for the prison, which were landed on a nearby wharf. This roustabout crew had all the unloading to do, and the reason I liked it was it gave us some chance to steal. Whenever there was anything extra, intended for the officers, to be unloaded, look out for accidents. Broken crates were common, and some of the contents was certain to reach our pockets or stomachs, in spite of the guard.

"I was a willing worker and stood well with the guards. They never searched me, and when they took us outside the stockade, the captain of the guard gave me permission, after our work was over, to patronize the sutler's store and buy knickknacks from the booths. There was always some little money amongst soldiers, even in prison, and I was occasionally furnished money by my messmates to buy bread from a baker's wagon which was outside the walls. Well, after I had traded a few times with the baker's boy, I succeeded in corrupting him. Yes, had him stealing from his employer and selling to me at a discount. I was a good customer, and being a prisoner, there was no danger of my meeting his employer. You see, the loaves were counted out to him, and he had to return the equivalent or the bread. At first the bread cost me ten cents for a small loaf, but when I got my scheme working, it didn't cost me five cents for the largest loaves the boy could steal from the bakery. I worked that racket for several months, and if we hadn't been exchanged, I'd have broke that baker, sure.

"But the most successful scheme I worked was stealing the kidneys out of beef while we were handling it. It was some distance from the wharf to the warehouse, and when I'd get a hind quarter of beef on my shoulder, it was an easy trick to burrow my hand through the tallow and get a good grip on the kidney. Then when I'd throw the quarter down in the warehouse, it would be minus a kidney, which secretly found lodgment in a large pocket in the inside of my shirt. I was satisfied with one or two kidneys a day when I first worked the trick, but my mess caught on, and then I had to steal by wholesale to satisfy them. Some days, when the guards were too watchful, I couldn't get very many, and then again when things were lax, 'Elijah's Raven' would get a kidney for each man in our mess. With the regular allowance of rations and what I could steal, when the Texas troops were exchanged, our mess was ragged enough, but pig-fat and slick as weasels. Lord love you, but we were a great mess of thieves."

Bibleback's Christmas Beef

told by
John Officer

Nearly all of Flood's old men were with him again, several of whom were then in Forrest's camp. A fight occurred among a group of saddle horses tied to the front wheel of the wagon, among them being the mount of John Officer. After the belligerents had been quieted, and Officer had removed and tied his horse to a convenient tree, he came over and joined our group, among which were the six trail bosses. Throwing himself down among us, and using Sponsilier for a pillow and myself for a footstool, he began to talk.

"All you foremen who have been over the Chisholm Trail remember the stage stand called Bull Foot, but possibly some of the boys haven't. Well, no matter, it's just about midway between Little Turkey Creek and Buffalo Springs on that trail, where it runs through the Cherokee Strip. I worked one year in that northern country—lots of Texas boys there too. It was just about the time they began to stock that country with Texas steers, and we rode lines to keep our cattle on their range. You bet, there was riding to do in that country then. The first few months that these Southern steers are turned loose on a new range, Lord! but they do love to drift against a breeze. In any kind of a rainstorm, they'll travel farther in a night than a whole outfit can turn them back in a day.

"Our camp was on the Salt Fork of the Cimarron, and late in the fall when all the beeves had been shipped, the outfit were riding lines and loose-herding a lot of Texas yearlings, and mixed cattle, natives to that range. Up in that country they have Indian summer and squaw winter, both occurring in the fall. They have lots of funny weather up there. Well, late one evening that fall there came an early squall of squaw winter, sleeted and spit snow wickedly. The next morning there wasn't a hoof in sight, and shortly after daybreak we were riding deep in our saddles to catch the lead drift of our cattle. After a hard day's ride, we found that we were out several hundred head, principally yearlings of the through Texas stock. You all know how locoed a bunch of dogies can get—we hunted for three days and for fifty miles in every direction, and neither hide, hair, nor hoof could we find. It was while we were hunting these cattle that my yarn commences.

"The big augers of the outfit lived in Wichita, Kansas. Their foreman, Bibleback Hunt, and myself were returning from hunting this missing bunch of yearlings when night overtook us, fully twenty-five miles from camp. Then this Bull Foot stage came to mind, and we turned our horses and rode to it. It was nearly dark when we reached it, and Bibleback said for me to go in and make the talk. I'll never forget that nice little woman who met me at the door of that sod shack. I told her our situation, and she seemed awfully gracious in granting us food and shelter for the night. She told us we could either picket our horses or put them in the corral and feed them hay and grain from the stage company's supply. Now, old Bibleback was what you might call shy of women, and steered clear of the house until she sent her little boy out and asked us to come in. Well, we sat around in the room, owly-like, and to save my soul from the wrath to come, I couldn't think of a word that was proper to say to the little woman, busy getting supper. Bibleback was worse off than I was; he couldn't do anything but look at the pictures on the wall. What was worrying me was, had she a husband? Or what was she doing away out there in that lonesome country? Then a man old enough to be her grandfather put in an appearance. He was friendly and quite talkative, and I built right up to him. And then we had a supper that I distinctly remember yet. Well, I should say I do—it takes a woman to get a good supper, and cheer it with her presence, sitting at the head of the table and pouring the coffee.

"This old man was a retired stage driver, and was doing the wrangling act for the stage horses. After supper I went out to the corral and wormed the information out of him that the woman was a widow; that her husband had died before she came there, and that she was from Michigan. Amongst other things that I learned from the old man was that she had only been there a few months, and was a poor but deserving woman. I told Bibleback all this after we had gone to bed, and we found that our finances amounted to only four dollars, which she was more than welcome to. So the next morning after breakfast, when I asked her what I owed her for our trouble, she replied graciously, 'Why, gentlemen, I couldn't think of taking advantage of your necessity to charge you for a favor that I'm only too happy to grant.'

" 'Oh,' said I, 'take this, anyhow,' laying the silver on the corner of the table, and starting for the door, when she stopped me.

" 'One moment, sir; I can't think of accepting this. Be kind enough to grant my request,' and returned the money.

"We mumbled out some thanks, bade her good day, and started for the corral, feeling like two sheep thieves. While we were saddling up—will you believe it?—her little boy came out to the corral and gave each one of us as fine a cigar as ever I buttoned my lip over. Well, fellows, we had had it put all over us by this little Michigan woman, till we couldn't look each other in the face. We were accustomed to hardship and neglect, but here was genuine kindness enough to kill a cat.

"Until we got within five miles of our camp that morning, old Bibleback wouldn't speak to me as we rode along. Then he turned halfway in his saddle and said, 'What kind of folks are those?'

" 'I don't know,' I replied, 'what kind of people they are, but I know they are good ones.'

" 'Well, I'll get even with that little woman if it takes every sou in my war bags,' said Hunt.

"When within a mile of camp, Bibleback turned again in his saddle and asked, 'When is Christmas?'

" 'In about five weeks,' I answered.

" 'Do you know where that big Wyoming stray ranges?' he next asked.

"I trailed onto his game in a second. 'Of course I do.'

" 'Well,' says he, 'let's kill him for Christmas and give that little widow every ounce of the meat. It'll be a good one on her, won't it? We'll fool her a-plenty. Say nothing to the others,' he added; and giving our horses the rein we rode into camp on a gallop.

"Three days before Christmas we drove up this Wyoming stray and beefed him. We hung the beef up overnight to harden in the frost, and the next morning bright and early, we started for the stage stand with a good pair of ponies to a light wagon. We reached the widow's place about eleven o'clock, and against her protests that she had no use for so much, we hung up eight hundred pounds of as fine beef as you ever set your peepers on. We wished her a merry Christmas, jumped into the wagon, clucked to the ponies, and merely hit the high places getting away. When we got well out of sight of the house—well, I've seen mule colts play and kid goats cut up their antics; I've seen children that was frolicsome; but for a man with gray hair on his head, old Bibleback Hunt that day was the happiest mortal I ever saw. He talked to the horses; he sang songs; he played Injun; and that Christmas was a merry one, for the debt was paid and our little widow had beef to throw to the dogs. I never saw her again, but wherever she is tonight, if my prayer counts, may God bless her!"

Old Turk and the Slicker

told by
Dave Sponsilier

Early in the evening I had warned my boys that we would start on our return at ten o'clock. The hour was nearly at hand, and in reply to my inquiry if our portion of the beef had been secured, Jack Splann said that he had cut off half a loin, a side of ribs, and enough steak for breakfast. Splann and I tied the beef to our cantle strings, and when we returned to the group, Sponsilier was telling of the stampede of his herd in the Panhandle about a month before. "But that run wasn't a circumstance to one which I figured in once, and in broad daylight," concluded Dave. It required no encouragement to get the story; all we had to do was to give him time to collect his thoughts.

"Yes, it was in the summer of '73," he finally continued. "It was my first trip over the trail, and I naturally fell into position at the drag end of the herd. I was a green boy of about eighteen at the time, having never before been fifty miles from the ranch where I was born. The herd belonged to Major Hood, and our destination was Ellsworth, Kansas. In those days they generally worked oxen to the chuck wagons, as they were ready sale in the upper country, and in good demand for breaking prairie. I reckon there must have been a dozen yoke of work steers in our herd that year, and they were more trouble to me than all the balance of the cattle, for they were slothful and sinfully lazy. My vocabulary of profanity was worn to a frazzle before we were out a week, and those oxen didn't pay any more attention to a rope or myself than to the buzzing of a gnat.

"There was one big roan ox, called Turk, which we worked to the wagon occasionally, but in crossing the Arbuckle Mountains in the Indian Territory, he got tender-footed. Another yoke was substituted, and in a few days Turk was on his feet again. But he was a cunning rascal and had learned to soldier, and while his feet were sore, I favored him with sandy trails and gave him his own time. In fact, most of my duties were driving that one ox, while the other boys handled the herd.

When his feet got well—I had toadied and babied him so—he was plumb ruined. I begged the foreman to put him back in the chuck team, but the cook kicked on account of his well-known laziness, so Turk and I continued to adorn the rear of the column. I reckon the foreman thought it better to have Turk and me late than no dinner. I tried a hundred different schemes to instill ambition and self-respect into that ox, but he was an old dog and contented with his evil ways.

"Several weeks passed, and Turk and I became a standing joke with the outfit. One morning I made the discovery that he was afraid of a slicker. For just about a full half day I had the best of him, and several times he was out of sight in the main body of the herd. But he always dropped to the rear, and finally the slicker lost its charm to move him. In fact, he rather enjoyed having me fan him with it—it seemed to cool him. It was the middle of the afternoon, and Turk had dropped about a quarter mile to the rear, while I was riding along beside and throwing the slicker over him like a blanket. I was letting him carry it, and he seemed to be enjoying himself, switching his tail in appreciation, when the matted brush of his tail noosed itself over one of the riveted buttons on the slicker. The next switch brought the yellow 'fish' bumping on his heels, and emitting a blood-curdling bellow, he curved his tail and started for the herd.

"Just for a minute it tickled me to see old Turk getting such a wiggle on him, but the next moment my mirth turned to seriousness, and I tried to cut him off from the other cattle, but he beat me, bellowing bloody murder.

The slicker was sailing like a kite, and the rear cattle took fright and began bawling as if they had struck a fresh scent of blood. The scare flashed through the herd from rear to point, and hell began popping right then and there. The air filled with dust and the earth trembled with the running cattle. Not knowing which way to turn, I stayed right where I was—in the rear.

"As the dust lifted, I followed up, and about a mile ahead picked up my slicker, and shortly afterward found old Turk, grazing contentedly. With every man in the saddle, that herd ran seven miles and was only turned by the Cimarron River. It was nearly dark when I and the roan ox overtook the cattle. Fortunately none of the swing men had seen the cause of the stampede, and I attributed it to fresh blood, which the outfit believed. My verdant innocence saved my scalp that time, but years afterward I nearly lost it when I admitted to my old foreman what had caused the stampede that afternoon. But I was a trail boss then and had learned my lesson."

Rich in Hounds

told by
Quince Forrest's Wrangler

The repast barely concluded in time for the wranglers and first guard from Forrest's and my outfit to reach camp, catch night horses, bed the cattle, and excuse the herders, as supper was served only at the one wagon. The relieved ones, like eleventh-hour guests, came tearing in after darkness, and the tempting spread soon absorbed them. As the evening wore on, the loungers gathered in several circles, and the raconteur held sway. The fact that we were in a country in which game abounded suggested numerous stories. The delights of cat-hunting by night found an enthusiast in each one present. Every dog in our memory, back to early boyhood, was properly introduced and his best qualities applauded. Not only cat hounds but coon dogs had a respectful hearing.

"I remember a hound," said Forrest's wrangler, "which I owned when a boy back in Virginia. My folks lived in the foothills of the Blue Ridge Mountains in that state. We were just as poor as our poorest neighbors. But if there was any one thing that that section was rich in it was dogs, principally hounds. This dog of mine was four years old when I left home to go to Texas. Fine hound, swallow-marked, and when he opened on a scent you could always tell what it was that he was running. I never allowed him to run with packs, but generally used him in treeing coon, which pestered the cornfields during roasting-ear season and in the fall. Well, after I had been out in Texas about five years, I concluded to go back on a little visit to the old folks. There were no railroads within twenty miles of my home, and I had to hoof it that distance, so I arrived after dark. Of course, my return was a great surprise to my folks, and we sat up late telling stories about things out West. I had worked with cattle all the time, and had made one trip over the trail from Collin County to Abilene, Kansas.

"My folks questioned me so fast that they gave me no show to make any inquiries in return, but I finally eased one in and asked about my dog Keiser, and was tickled to hear that he was still living. I went out and called him, but he failed to show up, when Mother explained his absence by saying that he often went out hunting alone now, since there was none of us boys at home to hunt with him. They told me that he was no account any longer; that he had grown old and gray, and Father said he was too slow on trail to be of any use. I noticed that it was a nice damp night, and if my old dog had been there, I think I'd have taken a circle around the fields in the hope of hearing him sing once more. Well, we went back into the house, and after talking awhile longer, I climbed into the loft and went to bed.

"I didn't sleep very sound that night, and awakened several times. About an hour before daybreak, I awoke suddenly and imagined I heard a hound baying faintly in the distance. Finally I got up and opened the board window in the gable and listened. Say, boys, I knew that hound's baying as well as I know my own saddle. It was old Keiser, and he had something treed about a mile from the house, across a ridge over in some slashes. I slipped on my clothes, crept downstairs, and taking my old man's rifle out of the rack, started to him.

"It was as dark as a stack of black cats, but I knew every path and byway by heart. I followed the fields as far as I could, and later, taking into the timber, I had to go around a long swamp. An old beaver dam had once crossed the outlet of this marsh, and once I gained it, I gave a long yell to let the dog know that someone was coming. He answered me, and quite a little while before day broke I reached him. Did he know me? Why, he knew me as easy as the little boy knew his pap. Right now, I can't remember any simple thing in my whole life that moved me just as that little reunion of me and my dog, there in those woods that morning. Why, he howled with delight. He licked my face and hands and stood up on me with his wet feet and said just as plain as he could that he was glad to see me again. And I was glad to meet him, even though he did make me feel as mellow as a girl over a baby.

"Well, when daybreak came, I shot a nice big fat Mr. Zip Coon out of an old pin oak, and we started for home like old pardners. Old as he was, he played like a puppy around me, and when we came in sight of the house, he ran on ahead and told the folks what he had found. Yes, you bet he told them. He came near clawing all the clothing off them in his delight. That's one reason I always like a dog and a poor man—you can't question their friendship."

Uncle Dave Hapfinger in Heaven

told by
Waterwall

A circus was in progress on the other side of the wagon. From a large rock, Jake Blair was announcing the various acts and introducing the actors and actresses. Runt Pickett, wearing a skirt made out of a blanket and belted with a hobble, won the admiration of all as the only living lady lion tamer. When we resumed comfortable positions on our side of the commissary, a lad named Waterwall, one of Sponsilier's boys, took up the broken thread where Forrest's wrangler had left off.

"The greatest dog man I ever knew," said he, "lived on the Guadalupe River. His name was Dave Hapfinger, and he had the loveliest vagabond temperament of any man I ever saw. It mattered nothing what he was doing, all you had to do was to give old Dave a hint that you knew where there was fish to be caught, or a bee course to hunt, and he would stop the plow and go with you for a week if necessary. He loved hounds better than any man I ever knew. You couldn't confer greater favor than to give him a promising hound pup, or, seeking the same, ask for one of his raising. And he was such a good fellow. If anyone was sick in the neighborhood, Uncle Dave always had time to kill them a squirrel every day; and he could make a broth for a baby, or fry a young squirrel, in a manner that would make a sick man's mouth water.

"When I was a boy, I've laid around many a campfire this way and listened to old Dave tell stories. He was quite a humorist in his way, and possessed a wonderful memory. He could tell you the day of the month, thirty years before, when he went to mill one time and found a peculiar bird's nest on the way. Colonel Andrews, owner of several large plantations, didn't like Dave, and threatened to prosecute him once for cutting a bee tree on his land. If the evidence had been strong enough, I reckon the Colonel would. No doubt Uncle Dave was guilty, but mere suspicion isn't sufficient proof.

"Colonel Andrews was a haughty old fellow, blue-blooded and proud as a peacock, and about the only way Dave could get even with him was in his own mild, humorous way. One day at dinner at a neighboring log-rolling, when all danger of prosecution for cutting the bee tree had passed, Uncle Dave told of a recent dream of his, a pure invention.

" 'I dreamt,' said he, 'that Colonel Andrews died and went to heaven. There was an unusually big commotion at St. Peter's gate on his arrival. A troop of angels greeted him, still the Colonel seemed displeased at his reception. But the welcoming hosts humored him forward, and on nearing the throne, the Almighty, recognizing the distinguished arrival, vacated the throne and came down to greet the Colonel personally. At this mark of appreciation, he relaxed a trifle, and when the Almighty insisted that he should take the throne seat, Colonel Andrews actually smiled for the first time on earth or in heaven.'

"Uncle Dave told this story so often that he actually believed it himself. But finally a wag friend of Colonel Andrews told of a dream which he had had about old Dave, which the latter hugely enjoyed. According to this second vagary, the old vagabond had also died and gone to heaven. There was some trouble at St. Peter's gate, as they refused to admit dogs, and Uncle Dave always had a troop of hounds at his heels. When he found that it was useless to argue the matter, he finally yielded the point and left the pack outside. Once inside the gate he stopped, bewildered at the scene before him. But after waiting inside some little time unnoticed, he turned and was on the point of asking the gatekeeper to let him out, when an angel approached and asked him to stay. There was some doubt in Dave's mind if he would like the place, but the messenger urged that he remain and at least look the city over. The old hunter good-naturedly consented, and as they started up one of the golden streets Uncle Dave recognized an old friend who had once given him a hound pup. Excusing himself to the angel, he rushed over to his former earthly friend and greeted him with warmth and cordiality. The two old cronies talked and talked about the things below, and finally Uncle Dave asked if there was any hunting up there. The reply was disappointing.

"Meanwhile the angel kept urging Uncle Dave forward to salute the throne. But he loitered along, meeting former hunting acquaintances, and stopping with each for a social chat. When they finally neared the throne, the patience of the angel was nearly exhausted; and as old Dave looked up and saw Colonel Andrews occupying the throne, he rebelled and refused to salute, when the angel wrathfully led him back to the gate and kicked him out among his dogs."

Jack Splann told a yarn about the friendship of a pet lamb and a dog which he owned when a boy. It was so unreasonable that he was interrupted on nearly every assertion. Long before he had finished, Sponsilier checked his narrative and informed him that if he insisted on doling out fiction he must have some consideration for his listeners, and at least tell it within reason. Splann stopped right there and refused to conclude his story, though no one but myself seemed to regret it. I had a true incident about a dog which I expected to tell, but the audience had become too critical, and I kept quiet.

The Marshal of Cow Springs

told by
a Cattle Buyer from Kansas City

It was a wet, bad year on the old Western Trail. From Red River north and all along was herd after herd waterbound by high water in the rivers. We were expected to arrive in Dodge early in June, but when we reached the North Fork of the Canadian, we were two weeks behind time. Old George Carter, the owner of the herd, was growing impatient about us, for he had had no word from us after we had crossed Red River at Doan's Crossing. Our surprise when we came opposite Camp Supply to have Carter and a stranger ride out to meet us was not to be measured. They had got impatient waiting, and had taken the mail buckboard to Supply, making inquiries along the route for the Hat herd, which had not passed up the trail, so they were assured. Carter was so impatient that he could not wait, as he had a prospective buyer on his hands. Old George was as tickled as a little boy to meet us all.

With the cattle on hand, drinking was out of the question, so the only way to show us any regard was to bring us a box of cigars. He must have brought those cigars from Texas, for they were wrapped in a copy of the *Fort Worth Gazette.* It was a month old and full of news. Every man in the outfit read and reread it. There were several train robberies reported in it, but that was common in those days. They had nominated for governor "The Little Cavalryman," Sul Ross, and this paper estimated that his majority would be at least two hundred thousand. We were all anxious to get home in time to vote for him.

That night around camp the smoke was curling upward from those cigars in clouds. When supper was over and the guards arranged for the night, storytelling was in order. This cattle buyer with us lived in Kansas City and gave us several good ones. He told us of an attempted robbery of a bank which had occurred a few days before in a western town.

"Cow Springs, Kansas," said he, "earned the reputation honestly of being a hard cowtown. When it became the terminus of one of the many eastern trails, it was at its worst. The death rate amongst its city marshals—always due to a six-shooter in the hands of some man who never hesitated to use it—made the office not overdesirable. The office was vacated so frequently in this manner that at last no local man could be found who would have it. Then the city fathers sent to Texas for a man who had the reputation of being a killer. He kept his record a vivid green by shooting first and asking questions afterward.

"Well, the first few months he filled the office of marshal he killed two white men and an Indian, and had the people thoroughly buffaloed. When the cattle season had ended and winter came on, the little town grew tame and listless. There was no man to dare him to shoot, and he longed for other worlds to conquer. He had won his way into public confidence with his little gun. But this confidence reposed in him was misplaced, for he proved his own double both in morals and courage.

"To show you the limit of the confidence he enjoyed: the treasurer of the Cherokee Strip Cattle Association paid rent money to that tribe, at their capital, fifty thousand dollars quarterly. The capital is not located on any railroad; so the funds in currency were taken in regularly by the treasurer, and turned over to the tribal authorities. This trip was always made with secrecy, and the marshal was taken along as a trusted guard. It was an extremely dangerous trip to make, as it was through a country infested with robbers and the capital at least a hundred miles from the railroad. Strange no one ever attempted to rob the stage or private conveyance, though this sum was taken in regularly for several years. The average robber was careful of his person, and could not be induced to make a target of himself for any money consideration, where there was danger of a gun in the hands of a man that would shoot rapidly and carelessly.

"Before the herds began to reach as far north, the marshal and his deputy gave some excuse and disappeared for a few days, which was quite common and caused no comment. One fine morning the good people of the town where the robbery was attempted were thrown into an uproar by shooting in their bank, just at the opening hour. The robbers were none other than our trusted marshal, his deputy, and a cowpuncher who had been led into the deal. When they ordered the officials of the bank to stand in a row with hands up, they were nonplused at their refusal to comply. The attacked party unearthed ugly-looking guns and opened fire on the holdups instead.

"This proved bad policy, for when the smoke cleared away, the cashier, a very popular man, was found dead, while an assistant was dangerously wounded. The shooting, however, had aroused the town to the situation, and men were seen running to and fro with guns. This unexpected refusal and the consequent shooting spoiled the plans of the robbers, so that they abandoned the robbery and ran to their horses.

"After mounting they parleyed with each other a moment and seemed bewildered as to which way they should ride, finally riding south toward what seemed a broken country. Very few minutes elapsed before every man who could find a horse was joining the posse that was forming to pursue them. Before they were out of sight the posse had started after them. They were well mounted and as determined a set of men as were ever called upon to meet a similar emergency. They had the decided advantage of the robbers, as their horses were fresh, and the men knew every foot of the country.

"The broken country to which the holdups headed was a delusion as far as safety was concerned. They were never for a moment out of sight of the pursuers, and this broken country ended in a deep coulee. When the posse saw them enter this they knew that their capture was only a matter of time. Nature seemed against the robbers, for as they entered the coulee their horses bogged down in a springy rivulet, and they were so hard pressed that they hastily dismounted, and sought shelter in some shrubbery that grew about. The pursuing party, now swollen to quite a number, had spread out and by this time surrounded the men. They were seen to take shelter in a clump of wild plum brush, and the posse closed in on them. Seeing the numbers against them, they came out on demand and surrendered. Neither the posse nor themselves knew at this time that the shooting in the bank had killed the cashier. Less than an hour's time had elapsed between the shooting and the capture. When the posse reached town on their return, they learned of the death of the cashier, and the identity of the prisoners was soon established by citizens who knew the marshal and his deputy. The latter admitted their identity.

"That afternoon they were photographed, and later in the day were given a chance to write to any friends to whom they wished to say good-by. The cowpuncher was the only one who availed himself of the opportunity. He wrote to his parents. He was the only one of the trio who had the nerve to write, and seemed the only one who realized the enormity of his crime, and that he would never see the sun of another day.

"As darkness settled over the town, the mob assembled. There was no demonstration. The men were taken quietly out and hanged. At the final moment there was a remarkable variety of nerve shown. The marshal and deputy were limp, unable to stand on their feet. With piteous appeals and tears they pleaded for mercy, something they themselves had never shown their own victims. The boy who had that day written his parents his last letter met his fate with Indian stoicism. He cursed the crouching figures of his pardners for enticing him into this crime, and begged them not to die like curs, but to meet bravely the fate which he admitted they all deserved. Several of the men in the mob came forward and shook hands with him, and with no appeal to man or his Maker, he was swung into the great unknown at the end of a rope. Such nerve is seldom met in life, and those that are supposed to have it, when they come face to face with their end, are found lacking that quality. It is a common anomaly in life that the bad man with his record often shows the white feather when he meets his fate at the hands of an outraged community."

We all took a friendly liking to the cattle buyer. He

was an interesting talker. While he was a city man, he mixed with us with a certain freedom and abandon that was easy and natural.

Trust and Betrayal

told by
Bat Shaw

"I've heard my father tell about those Cherokees," said Port Cole. "They used to live in Georgia, those Indians. They must have been honest people, for my father told us boys at home, that once in the old state while the Cherokees lived there, his father hired one of their tribe to guide him over the mountains. There was a pass through the mountains that was used and known only to these Indians. It would take six weeks to go and come, and to attend to the business in view. My father was a small boy at the time, and says that his father hired the guide for the entire trip for forty dollars in gold. One condition was that the money was to be paid in advance. The morning was set for the start, and my grandfather took my father along on the trip.

"Before starting from the Indian's cabin my grandfather took out his purse and paid the Indian four ten-dollar gold pieces. The Indian walked over to the corner of the cabin, and in the presence of other Indians laid this gold, in plain sight of all, on the end of a log that projected where they cross outside, and got on his horse to be gone six weeks. They made the trip on time, and my father said his first thought, on their return to the Indian village, was to see if the money was untouched. It was. You couldn't risk white folks that way."

"Oh, I don't know," said one of the boys. "Suppose you save your wages this summer and try it next year when we start up the trail, just to see how it will work."

"Well, if it's just the same to you," replied Port, lighting a fresh cigar, "I'll not try, for I'm well enough satisfied as to how it would turn out, without testing it."

"Isn't it strange," said Bat Shaw, "that if you trust a man or put confidence in him he won't betray you. Now, that marshal—one month he was guarding money at the risk of his life, and the next was losing his life trying to rob someone. I remember a similar case down on the Rio Grande. It was during the boom in sheep a few years ago, when everyone got crazy over sheep.

"A couple of Americans came down on the river to

buy sheep. They brought their money with them. It was before the time of any railroads. The man they deposited their money with had lived amongst these Mexicans till he had forgotten where he did belong, though he was a Yankee. These sheep buyers asked their banker to get them a man who spoke Spanish and knew the country, as a guide. The banker sent and got a man that he could trust. He was a swarthy-looking native whose appearance would not recommend him anywhere. He was accepted, and they set out to be gone over a month.

"They bought a band of sheep, and it was necessary to pay for them at a point some forty miles farther up the river. There had been some robbing along the river, and these men felt uneasy about carrying the money to this place to pay for the sheep. The banker came to the rescue by advising them to send the money by the Mexican, who could take it through in a single night. No one would ever suspect him of ever having a dollar on his person. It looked risky, but the banker who knew the nature of the native urged it as the better way, assuring them that the Mexican was perfectly trustworthy. The peon was brought in, the situation was explained to him, and he was ordered to be in readiness at nightfall to start on his errand.

"He carried the money over forty miles that night, and delivered it safely in the morning to the proper parties. This act of his aroused the admiration of these sheepmen beyond a point of safety. They paid for the sheep, were gone for a few months, sold out their flocks to good advantage, and came back to buy more. This second time they did not take the precaution to have the banker hire the man, but did so themselves, intending to deposit their money with a different house farther up the river. They confided to him that they had quite a sum of money with them, and that they would deposit it with the same merchant to whom he had carried the money before.

"The first night they camped, the Mexican murdered them both, took the money, and crossed into Mexico. He hid their bodies, and it was months before they were missed, and a year before their bones were found. He had plenty of time to go to the ends of the earth before his crime would be discovered.

"Now that Mexican would never think of betraying the banker, his old friend and patron, his *muy buen amigo*. There were obligations that he could not think of breaking with the banker; but these fool sheepmen, supposing it was simple honesty, paid the penalty of their confidence with their lives. Now, when he rode over this same road alone, a few months before, with over five thousand dollars in money belonging to these same men, all he would need to have done was to ride across the river. When there were no obligations binding, he was willing to add murder to robbery. Some folks say that Mexicans are good people; it is the climate, possibly, but they can always be depended on to assay high in treachery."

The Owner of the Pinto Horse

told by
George Carter

"What guard are you going to put me on to-night?" inquired old man Carter of Baugh.

"This outfit," said Baugh, in reply, "don't allow any tenderfoot around the cattle—at night, at least. You'd better play you're company; somebody that's come. If you're so very anxious to do something, the cook may let you rustle wood or carry water. We'll fix you up a bed after a little, and see that you get into it where you can sleep and be harmless.

"Colonel," added Baugh, "why is it that you never tell that experience you had once amongst the greasers?"

"Well, there was nothing funny in it to me," said Carter, "and they say I never tell it twice alike."

"Why, certainly, tell us," said the cattle buyer. "I've never heard it. Don't throw off tonight."

"It was a good many years ago," began old man George, "but the incident is very clear in my mind. I was working for a month's wages then myself. We were driving cattle out of Mexico. The people I was working for contracted for a herd down in Chihuahua, about four hundred miles south of El Paso. We sent in our own outfit—wagon, horses, and men—two weeks before. I was kept behind to take in the funds to pay for the cattle. The day before I started, my people drew out of the bank twenty-eight thousand dollars, mostly large bills. They wired ahead and engaged a rig to take me from the station where I left the railroad to the ranch, something like ninety miles.

"I remember I bought a new moleskin suit, which was very popular then. I had nothing but a small handbag, and it contained only a six-shooter. I bought a book to read on the train and on the road out, called *Other People's Money.* The title caught my fancy, and it was very interesting. It was written by a Frenchman—full of love and thrilling situations. I had the money belted on me securely, and started out with flying colors. The railroad runs through a dreary country, not worth a second look, so I read my new book. When I arrived at the station I found the conveyance awaiting me. The plan was to drive halfway, and stay overnight at a certain hacienda.

"The driver insisted on starting at once, telling me that we could reach the Hacienda Grande by ten o'clock that night, which would be half my journey. We had a double-seated buckboard and covered the country rapidly. There were two Mexicans on the front seat, while I had the rear one all to myself. Once on the road I interested myself in *Other People's Money,* almost forgetful of the fact that at that very time I had enough of other people's money on my person to set all the bandits in Mexico on my trail. There was nothing of incident that evening, until an hour before sundown. We reached a small ranchito, where we spent an hour changing horses, had coffee and a rather light lunch.

"Before leaving I noticed a pinto horse hitched to a tree some distance in the rear of the house, and as we were expecting to buy a number of horses, I walked back and looked this one carefully over. He was very peculiarly color-marked in the mane. I inquired for his owner, but they told me that he was not about at present. It was growing dusk when we started out again. The evening was warm and sultry and threatening rain. We had been on our way about an hour when I realized we had left the main road and were bumping along on a byroad. I asked the driver his reason for this, and he explained that it was a cutoff, and that by taking it we would save three miles and half an hour's time. As a further reason he expressed his opinion that we would have rain that night, and that he was anxious to reach the hacienda in good time. I encouraged him to drive faster, which he did. Within another hour I noticed we were going down a dry arroyo, with mesquite brush on both sides of the road, which was little better than a trail. My suspicions were never aroused sufficiently to open the little handbag and belt on the six-shooter. I was dreaming along when we came to a sudden stop before what seemed a deserted jacal. The Mexicans mumbled something to each other over some disappointment, when the driver said to me, 'Here's where we stay all night. This is the hacienda.'

"They both got out and insisted on my getting out, but I refused to do so. I reached down and picked up my little grip and was in the act of opening it, when one of them grabbed my arm and jerked me out of the seat to the ground. I realized then for the first time that I was in for it in earnest. I never knew before that I could put up such a fine defense, for inside a minute I had them both blinded in their own blood. I gathered up rocks and had them flying when I heard a clatter of hoofs coming down the arroyo like a squadron of cavalry. They were so close on to me that I took to the brush, without hat, coat, or pistol. Men that pack a gun all their lives never have it when they need it; that was exactly my fix. Darkness was in my favor, but I had no more idea where I was or which way I was going than a baby. One thing sure, I was trying to get away from there as fast as I could. The night was terribly dark, and about ten o'clock it began to rain a deluge. I kept going all night, but must have been circling.

"Towards morning I came to an arroyo which was running full of water. My idea was to get that between me and the scene of my trouble, so I took off my boots to wade it. When about one-third way across, I either stepped off a bluff bank or into a well, for I went under and dropped the boots. When I came to the surface I made a few strokes swimming and landed in a clump of mesquite brush, to which I clung, got on my feet, and waded out to the opposite bank more scared than hurt. Right there I lay until daybreak.

"The thing that I remember best now was the peculiar odor of the wet moleskin. If there had been a strolling artist about looking for a picture of Despair, I certainly would have filled the bill. The sleeves were torn out of my shirt, and my face and arms were scratched and bleeding from the thorns of the mesquite. No one who could have seen me then would ever have dreamed that I was a walking depositary of 'other people's money.' When it got good daylight I started out and kept the shelter of the brush to hide me. After nearly an hour's travel, I came out on a divide, and about a mile off I saw what looked like a jacal. Directly I noticed a smoke arise, and I knew then it was a habitation. My appearance was not what I desired, but I approached it.

"In answer to my knock at the door a woman opened it about two inches and seemed to be more interested in examination of my anatomy than in listening to my troubles. After I had made an earnest, sincere talk she asked me, 'No está loco?' I assured her that I was perfectly sane, and that all I needed was food and clothing, for which I would pay her well. It must have been my appearance that aroused her sympathy, for she admitted me and fed me.

"The woman had a little girl of probably ten years of age. This little girl brought me water to wash myself, while the mother prepared me something to eat. I was so anxious to pay these people that I found a five-dollar gold piece in one of my pockets and gave it to the little girl, who in turn gave it to her mother. While I was drinking the coffee and eating my breakfast, the woman saw me looking at a picture of the Virgin Mary which was hanging on the adobe wall opposite me. She asked me if I was a Catholic, which I admitted. Then she brought out a shirt and offered it to me.

"Suddenly the barking of a dog attracted her to the door. She returned breathless, and said in good Spanish: 'For God's sake, run! Fly! Don't let my husband and brother catch you here, for they are coming home.' She thrust the shirt into my hand and pointed out the direction in which I should go. From a concealed point of the brush I saw two men ride up to the jacal and dismount. One of them was riding the pinto horse I had seen the day before.

"I kept the brush for an hour or so, and finally came out on the mesa. Here I found a flock of sheep and a *pastor*. From this shepherd I learned that I was about ten miles from the main road. He took the sandals from his own feet and fastened them on mine, gave me directions, and about night I reached the hacienda, where I was kindly received and cared for. This ranchero sent after officers and had the country scoured for the robbers. I was detained nearly a week, to see if I could identify my drivers, without result. They even brought in the owner of the pinto horse, and no doubt husband of the woman who saved my life.

"After a week's time I joined our own outfit, and I never heard a language that sounded so sweet as the English of my own tongue. I would have gone back and testified against the owner of the spotted horse if it hadn't been for a woman and a little girl who depended on him, robber that he was."

He Had Collided with Lead in Texas

told by
Theodore Baughman

"Now, girls," said Baugh, addressing Carter and the stranger, "I've made you a bed out of the wagon sheet, and rustled a few blankets from the boys. You'll find the bed under the wagon tongue, and we've stretched a fly over it to keep the dew off you, besides adding privacy to your apartments. So you can turn in when you run out of stories or get sleepy."

"Haven't you got one for us?" inquired the cattle buyer of Baugh. "This is no time to throw off, or refuse to be sociable."

"Well, now, that bank robbery that you were telling the boys about," said Baugh, as he bit the tip from a fresh cigar, "reminds me of a holdup that I was in up in the San Juan mining country in Colorado. We had driven into that mining camp a small bunch of beef and had sold them to fine advantage. The outfit had gone back, and I remained behind to collect for the cattle, expecting to take the stage and overtake the outfit down on the river. I had neglected to book my passage in advance, so when the stage was ready to start I had to content myself with a seat on top. I don't remember the amount of money I had. It was the proceeds of something like one hundred and fifty beeves, in a small bag along of some old clothes. There wasn't a cent of it mine, still I was supposed to look after it.

"The driver answered to the name of Southpaw, drove six horses, and we had a jolly crowd on top. Near midnight we were swinging along, and as we rounded a turn in the road, we noticed a flickering light ahead some distance which looked like the embers of a campfire. As we came nearly opposite the light, the leaders shied at some object in the road in front of them. Southpaw uncurled his whip, and was in the act of pouring the leather into them, when that light was uncovered as big as the headlight of an engine. An empty five-gallon oil can had been cut in half and used as a reflector, throwing full light into the road sufficient to cover the entire coach. Then came a round of orders which meant business. 'Shoot them leaders if they cross that obstruction!' 'Kill anyone that gets off on the opposite side!' 'Driver, move up a few feet farther!' 'A few feet farther, please.' 'That'll do; thank you, sir.' 'Now, every son-of-a-horse-thief, get out on this side of the coach, please, and be quick about it!'

"The man giving these orders stood a few feet behind the lamp and out of sight, but the muzzle of a Winchester was plainly visible and seemed to cover every man on the stage. It is needless to say that we obeyed, got down in the full glare of the light, and lined up with our backs to the robber, hands in the air. There was a heavily veiled woman on the stage, whom he begged to hold the light for him, assuring her that he never robbed a woman. This veiled person disappeared at the time, and was supposed to have been a confederate. When the light was held for him, he drew a black cap over each one of us, searching everybody for weapons. Then he proceeded to rob us, and at last went through the mail. It took him over an hour to do the job; he seemed in no hurry.

"It was not known what he got out of the mail, but the passengers yielded about nine hundred revenue to him, while there was three times that amount on top the coach in my grip, wrapped in a dirty flannel shirt. When he disappeared we were the cheapest lot of men imaginable. It was amusing to hear the excuses, threats, and the like; but the fact remained the same, that a dozen of us had been robbed by a lone highwayman. I felt good over it, as the money in the grip had been overlooked.

"Well, we cleared out the obstruction in the road, and got aboard the coach once more. About four o'clock in the morning we arrived at our destination, only two hours late. In the hotel office where the stage stopped was the very man who had robbed us. He had got in an hour ahead of us, and was a very much interested listener to the incident as retold. There was an early train out of town that morning, and at a place where they stopped for breakfast he sat at the table with several drummers who were in the holdup, a most attentive listener.

"He was captured the same day. He had hired a horse out of a livery stable the day before, to ride out to look at a ranch he thought of buying. The liveryman noticed that he limped slightly. He had collided with lead in Texas, as was learned afterward. The horse which had been hired to the ranch buyer of the day before was returned to the corral of the livery barn at an unknown hour during the night, and suspicion settled on the lame man. When he got off the train at Pueblo, he walked into the arms of officers. The limp had marked him clearly.

"In a grip which he carried were a number of sacks, which he supposed contained gold dust, but held only talc on its way to assayers in Denver. These he had gotten out of the express the night before, supposing they were valuable. We were all detained as witnesses. He was tried for robbing the mails, and was the coolest man in the courtroom. He was a tall, awkward-looking fellow, light-complexioned, with a mild blue eye. His voice, when not disguised, would mark him amongst a thousand men. It was peculiarly mild and soft, and would lure a babe from its mother's arms.

"At the trial he never tried to hide his past, and you couldn't help liking the fellow for his frank answers.

" 'Were you ever charged with any crime before?' asked the prosecution. 'If so, when and where?'

" 'Yes,' said the prisoner, 'in Texas, for robbing the mails in '77.'

" 'What was the result?' continued the prosecution.

" 'They sent me over the road for ninety-nine years.'

" 'Then how does it come that you are at liberty?' quizzed the attorney.

" 'Well, you see the President of the United States at that time was a warm personal friend of mine, though we had drifted apart somewhat. When he learned that the federal authorities had interfered with my liberties, he pardoned me out instantly.'

" 'What did you do then?' asked the attorney.

" 'Well, I went back to Texas, and was attending to my own business, when I got into a little trouble and had to kill a man. Lawyers down there won't do anything for you without you have money, and as I didn't have any for them, I came up to this country to try and make an honest dollar.'

"He went over the road a second time, and wasn't in the federal prison a year before he was released through influence. Prison walls were never made to hold as cool a rascal as he was. Have you a match?"

Alkaline Dust Ain't Snow

told by
Ace Gee

The evening before the Cherokee Strip was thrown open for settlement, a number of old-timers met in the little town of Hennessey, Oklahoma.

On the next day the Strip would pass from us and our employers, the cowmen. Some of the boys had spent from five to fifteen years on this range. But we realized that we had come to the parting of the ways. This country had been a home to us. It mattered little if our names were on the payroll or not—it had clothed and fed us.

We were seated around a table in the rear of a saloon talking of the morrow. The place was run by a former cowboy. It therefore became a rendezvous for the craft. Most of us had made up our minds to quit cattle for good and take claims.

"Before I take a claim," said Tom Roll, "I'll go to Minnesota and peon myself to some Swede farmer for my keep the balance of my life. Making hay and plowing fireguards the last few years have given me all the taste of farming that I want. I'm going to Montana in the spring."

"Why don't you go this winter? Is your underwear too light?" asked Ace Gee. "Now, I'm going to make a farewell play," continued Ace. "I'm going to take a claim, and before I file on it, sell my rights, go back to old Van Zandt County, Texas, this winter, rear up my feet, and tell it to them scary. That's where all my folks live."

"Well, for a winter's stake," chimed in Joe Box, "Ace's scheme is all right. We can get five hundred dollars out of a claim for simply staking it, and we know some good ones. That sized roll ought to winter a man with modest tastes."

"You didn't know that I just came from Montana, did you, Tom?" asked Ace. "I can tell you more about that country than you want to know. I've been up the trail this year; delivered our cattle on the Yellowstone, where the outfit I worked for has a northern range. When I remember this summer's work, I sometimes think that I will burn my saddle and never turn or look a cow in the face again, nor ride anything but a plow mule and that bareback.

"The people I was working for have a range in Tom Green County, Texas, and another one in Montana. They send their young steers north to mature—good idea, too!—but they are not cowmen like the ones we know. They made their money in the East in a patent medicine—got scads of it, too. But that's no argument that they know anything about a cow. They have a board of directors—it is one of those cattle companies. Looks like they started in the cattle business to give their income a healthy outlet from the medicine branch. They operate on similar principles as those soap factory people did here in the Strip a few years ago. About the time they learn the business they go broke and retire.

"Our boss this summer was some relation to the wife of some of the medicine people down East. As they had no use for him back there, they sent him out to the ranch, where he would be useful.

"We started north with the grass. Had thirty-three hundred head of twos and threes, with a fair string of saddle stock. They run the same brand on both ranges—the broken arrow. You never saw a cow boss have so much trouble; a married woman wasn't a circumstance to him, fretting and sweating continually. This was his first trip over the trail, but the boys were a big improvement on the boss, as we had a good outfit of men along. My idea of a good cow boss is a man that doesn't boss any; just hires a first-class outfit of men, and then there is no bossing to do.

"'We had to keep well to the west getting out of Texas; kept to the west of Buffalo Gap. From there to Tepee City is a dry, barren country. To get water for a herd the size of ours was some trouble. This new medicine man got badly worried several times. He used his draft book freely, buying water for the cattle while crossing this stretch of desert; the natives all through there considered him the softest snap they had met in years. Several times we were without water for the stock two whole days. That makes cattle hard to hold at night. They want to get up and prowl—it makes them feverish, and then's when they are ripe for a stampede. We had several bobbles crossing that strip of country; nothing bad, just jump and run a mile or so, and then mill until daylight. Then our boss would get great action on himself and ride a horse until the animal would give out—sick, he called it. After the first little run we had, it took him half the next day to count them; then he couldn't believe his own figures.

"'A Val Verde County lad who counted with him said they were all right—not a hoof shy. But the medicine man's opinion was the reverse. At this the Val Verde boy got on the prod slightly, and expressed himself, saying, 'Why don't you have two of the other boys count them? You can't come within a hundred of me, or yourself either, for that matter. I can pick out two men, and if they differ five head, it'll be a surprise to me. The way the boys have brought the cattle by us, any man that can't count this herd and not have his own figures differ more than a hundred had better quit riding, get himself some sandals, and a job herding sheep. Let me give you this pointer: if you are not anxious to have last night's fun over again, you'd better quit counting and get this herd full of grass and water before night, or you will be cattle shy as sure as hell's hot.'

" 'When I ask you for an opinion,' answered the foreman, somewhat indignant, 'such remarks will be in order. Until then you may keep your remarks to yourself.'

" 'That will suit me all right, old sport,' retorted Val Verde; 'and when you want anyone to help you count your fat cattle, get some of the other boys—one that'll let you doubt his count as you have mine, and if he admires you for it, cut my wages in two.'

"After the two had been sparring with each other some little time, another of the boys ventured the advice that it would be easy to count the animals as they came out of the water; so the order went forward to let them hit the trail for the first water. We made a fine stream, watering early in the afternoon. As they grazed out from the creek we fed them through between two of the boys. The count showed no cattle short. In fact, the Val Verde boy's count was confirmed. It was then that our medicine man played his cards wrong. He still insisted that we were cattle out, thus queering himself with his men. He was gradually getting into a lone minority, though he didn't have sense enough to realize it. He would even fight with and curse his horses to impress us with his authority. Very little attention was paid to him after this, and as grass and water improved right along nothing of interest happened.

"While crossing 'No-Man's-Land' a month later—I was on herd myself at the time, a bright moonlight night —they jumped like a cat shot with No. 8's, and quit the bed-ground instanter. There were three of us on guard at the time, and before the other boys could get out of their blankets and into their saddles the herd had gotten well under headway. Even when the others came to our assistance, it took us some time to quiet them down. As this scare came during last guard, daylight was on us before they had quit milling, and we were three miles from the wagon. As we drifted them back towards camp, for fear that something might have gotten away, most of the boys scoured the country for miles about, but without reward. When all had returned to camp, had breakfasted and changed horses, the counting act was ordered by Mr. Medicine. Our foreman naturally felt that he would have to take a hand in this count, evidently forgetting his last experience in that line. He was surprised, when he asked one of the boys to help him, by receiving a flat refusal.

" 'Why won't you count with me?' he demanded.

" 'Because you don't possess common cow sense enough, nor is the crude material in you to make a cowhand. You found fault with the men the last count we had, and I don't propose to please you by giving you a chance to find fault with me. That's why I won't count with you.'

" 'Don't you know, sir, that I'm in authority here?' retorted the foreman.

" 'Well, if you are, no one seems to respect your authority, as you're pleased to call it, and I don't know of any reason why I should. You have plenty of men here who can count them correctly. I'll count them with any man in the outfit but yourself.'

" 'Our company sent me as their representative with this herd,' replied the foreman, 'while you have the insolence to disregard my orders. I'll discharge you the first moment I can get a man to take your place.'

" 'Oh, that'll be all right,' answered the lad, as the foreman rode away. He then tackled me, but I acted foolish, 'fessing up that I couldn't count a hundred. Finally he rode around to a quiet little fellow, with pockmarks on his face, who always rode on the point, kept his horses fatter than anybody, rode a San Jose saddle, and was called Californy. The boss asked him to help him count the herd.

" 'Now look here, boss,' said Californy, 'I'll pick one of the boys to help me, and we'll count the cattle to within a few head. Won't that satisfy you?'

" 'No, sir, it won't. What's got into you boys?' questioned the foreman.

" 'There's nothing the matter with the boys, but the cattle business has gone to the dogs when a valuable herd like this will be trusted to cross a country for two thousand miles in the hands of a man like yourself. You have men that will pull you through if you'll only let them,' said the point rider, his voice mild and kind as though he were speaking to a child.

" 'You're just like the rest of them!' roared the boss. 'Want to act contrary! Now let me say to you that you'll help me to count these cattle or I'll discharge, unhorse, and leave you afoot here in this country! I'll make an example of you as a warning to others.'

" 'It's strange that I should be signaled out as an object of your wrath and displeasure,' said Californy. 'Besides, if I were you, I wouldn't make any examples as you were thinking of doing. When you talk of making an example of me as a warning to others,' said the pock-marked lad, as he reached over, taking the reins of the foreman's horse firmly in his hand, 'you're a simpering idiot for entertaining the idea, and a cowardly bluffer for mentioning it. When you talk of unhorsing and leaving me here afoot in a country a thousand miles from nowhere, you don't know what that means, but there's no danger of your doing it. I feel easy on that point. But I'm sorry to see you make such a fool of yourself. Now, you may think for a moment that I'm afraid of that ivory-handled gun you wear, but I'm not. Men wear them on the range, not so much to emphasize their demands with, as you might think. If it were me, I'd throw it in the wagon; it may get you into trouble. One thing certain, if you ever so much as lay your hand on it, when you are making threats as you have done today, I'll build a fire in your face that you can read the *San Francisco Examiner* by at midnight. You'll have to revise your ideas a trifle; in fact, change your tactics. You're off your reservation bigger than a wolf, when you try to run things by force. There's lots better ways. Don't try and make talk stick for actions, nor use any prelude to the real play you wish to make. Unroll your little game with the real thing. You can't throw alkaline dust in my eyes and tell me it's snowing. I'm sorry to have to tell you all this, though I have noticed that you needed it for a long time.'

"As he released his grip on the bridle reins, he continued, 'Now ride back to the wagon, throw off that gun, tell some of the boys to take a man and count these cattle, and it will be done better than if you helped.'

" 'Must I continue to listen to these insults on every hand?' hissed the medicine man, livid with rage.

" 'First remove the cause before you apply the remedy; that's in your line,' answered Californy. 'Besides, what are you going to do about it? You don't seem to be gifted with enough cow sense to even use a modified amount of policy in your everyday affairs,' said he, as he rode away to avoid hearing his answer.

"Several of us, who were near enough to hear this dressing down of the boss at Californy's hands, rode up to offer our congratulations, when we noticed that old Bad Medicine had gotten a stand on one of the boys called Pink. After leaving him, he continued his ride towards the wagon. Pink soon joined us, a broad smile playing over his homely florid countenance.

" 'Some of you boys must have given him a heavy dose for so early in the morning,' said Pink, 'for he ordered me to have the cattle counted, and report to him at the wagon. Acted like he didn't aim to do the trick himself. Now, as I'm foreman,' continued Pink, 'I want you two point men to go up to the first little rise of ground, and we'll put the cattle through between you. I want a close count, understand. You're working under a boss now that will shove you through hell itself. So if you miss them over a hundred, I'll speak to the management, and see if I can't have your wages raised, or have you made a foreman or something with big wages and nothing to do.'

"The point men smiled at Pink's orders, and one asked, 'Are you ready now?'

" 'All set,' responded Pink. 'Let the fiddlers cut loose.'

"Well, we lined them up and got them strung out in shape to count, and our point men picking out a favorite rise, we lined them through between our counters. We fed them through, and as regularly as a watch you could hear Californy call out to his pardner, 'Tally!' Alternately they would sing out this check on the even hundred head, slipping a knot on their tally string to keep the hundreds. It took a full half hour to put them through, and when the rear guard of crips and dogies passed this impromptu review, we all waited patiently for the verdict. Our counters rode together, and Californy, leaning over on the pommel of his saddle, said to his pardner, 'What you got?'

" 'Thirty-three six,' was the answer.

" 'Why, you can't count a little bit,' said Californy. 'I got thirty-three seven. How does the count suit you, boss?'

" 'Easy suited, gents,' said Pink. 'But I'm surprised to find such good men with a common cow herd. I must try and have you appointed by the government on this commission that's to investigate Texas fever. You're altogether too accomplished for such a common calling as claims you at present.'

"'Turning to the rest of us, he said, 'Throw your cattle on the trail, you vulgar peons, while I ride back to order forward my wagon and saddle stock. By rights, I ought to have one of those center fire cigars to smoke, to set off my authority properly on this occasion.'

"He jogged back to the wagon and satisfied the dethroned medicine man that the cattle were there to a hoof. We soon saw the saddle horses following, and an hour afterward Pink and the foreman rode by us, big as fat cattle buyers from Kansas City, not even knowing anyone, so absorbed in their conversation were they; rode on by and up the trail, looking out for grass and water.

"It was over two weeks afterward when Pink said to us, 'When we strike the Santa Fe Railway, I may advise my man to take a needed rest for a few weeks in some of the mountain resorts. I hope you all noticed how worried he looks, and, to my judgment, he seems to be losing flesh. I don't like to suggest anything, but the day before we reach the railroad, I think a day's curlew shooting in the sand hills along the Arkansas River might please his highness. In case he'll go with me, if I don't lose him, I'll never come back to this herd. It won't hurt him any to sleep out one night with the dry cattle.'

"Sure enough, the day before we crossed that road, somewhere near the Colorado state line, Pink and Bad Medicine left camp early in the morning for a curlew hunt in the sand hills. Fortunately it was a foggy morning, and within half an hour the two were out of sight of camp and herd. As Pink had outlined the plans, everything was understood. We were encamped on a nice stream, and instead of trailing along with the herd, lay over for that day. Night came and our hunters failed to return, and the next morning we trailed forward towards the Arkansas River. Just as we went into camp at noon, two horsemen loomed up in sight coming down the trail from above. Every rascal of us knew who they were, and when the two rode up, Pink grew very angry and demanded to know why we had failed to reach the river the day before.

"The horse wrangler, a fellow named Joe George, had been properly coached, and stepping forward, volunteered this excuse: 'You all didn't know it when you left camp yesterday morning that we were out the wagon team and nearly half the saddle horses. Well, we were. And what's more, less than a mile below on the creek was an abandoned Indian camp. I wasn't going to be left behind with the cook to look for the missing stock, and told the *segundo* so. We divided into squads of three or four men each and went out and looked up the horses, but it was after six o'clock before we trailed them down and got the missing animals. If anybody thinks I'm going to stay behind to look for missing stock in a country full of lurking Indians—well, they simply don't know me.'

"The scheme worked all right. On reaching the railroad the next morning, Bad Medicine authorized Pink to take the herd to Ogallala on the Platte, while he took a train for Denver. Around the campfire that night, Pink gave us his experience in losing Mr. Medicine. 'Oh, I lost him late enough in the day so he couldn't reach any shelter for the night,' said Pink. 'At noon, when the sun was straight overhead, I sounded him as to directions and found that he didn't know straight up or east from west. After giving him the slip, I kept an eye on him among the sand hills, at the distance of a mile or so, until he gave up and unsaddled at dusk. The next morning when I overtook him, I pretended to be trailing him up, and I threw enough joy into my rapture over finding him, that he never doubted my sincerity.'

"On reaching Ogallala, a man from Montana put in an appearance in company with poor old Medicine, and as they did business strictly with Pink, we were left out of the grave and owly council of medicine men. Well, the upshot of the whole matter was that Pink was put in charge of the herd, and a better foreman I never worked under. We reached the company's Yellowstone range early in the fall, counted over and bade our dogies good-by, and rode into headquarters. That night I talked with the regular men on the ranch, and it was there that I found out that a first-class cowhand could get in four months' haying in the summer and the same feeding it out in the winter. But don't you forget it, she's a cow country all right. I always was such a poor hand afoot that I passed up that country, and here I am a 'boomer'."

"Well, boom if you want," said Tom Roll, "but do you all remember what the governor of North Carolina said to the governor of South Carolina?"

"It is quite a long time between drinks," remarked Joe, rising, "but I didn't want to interrupt Ace."

As we lined up at the bar, Ace held up a glass two-thirds full, and looking at it in a meditative mood, remarked, "Isn't it funny how little of this stuff it takes to make a fellow feel rich! Why, four bits' worth under his belt, and the President of the United States can't hire him."

As we strolled out into the street, Joe inquired, "Ace, where will I see you after supper?"

"You will see me, not only after supper, but all during supper, sitting right beside you."

Why the Chisholm Trail Forks

told by
Stubb

Early in the summer of '78 we were rocking along with a herd of Laurel Leaf cattle, going up the old Chisholm Trail in the Indian Territory. The cattle were in charge of Ike Inks as foreman, and had been sold for delivery somewhere in the Strip.

There were thirty-one hundred head, straight twos, and in the single ranch brand. We had been out about four months on the trail, and all felt that a few weeks at the farthest would let us out, for the day before we had crossed the Cimarron River, ninety miles south of the state line of Kansas.

The foreman was simply killing time, waiting for orders concerning the delivery of the cattle. All kinds of jokes were in order, for we all felt that we would soon be set free. One of our men had been taken sick, as we crossed Red River into the Nations, and not wanting to cross this Indian country shorthanded, Inks had picked up a young fellow who evidently had never been over the trail before. He gave the outfit his correct name, on joining us, but it proved unpronounceable, and for convenience someone rechristened him Lucy, as he had quite a feminine appearance. He was anxious to learn, and was in evidence in everything that went on.

The trail from the Cimarron to Little Turkey Creek, where we were now camped, had originally been to the east of the present one, skirting a blackjack country. After being used several years it had been abandoned, being sandy, and the new route followed up the bottoms of Big Turkey, since it was firmer soil, affording better footing to cattle. These two trails came together again at Little Turkey. At no place were they over two or three miles apart, and from where they separated to where they came together again was about seven miles.

It troubled Lucy not to know why this was thus. Why did these routes separate and come together again? He was fruitful with inquiries as to where this trail or that road led. The boss man had a vein of humor in his make-up, though it was not visible; so he told the young man that he did not know, as he had been over this route but once before, but he thought that Stubb, who was then on herd, could tell him how it was; he had been over the trail every year since it was laid out. This was sufficient to secure Stubb an interview, as soon as he was relieved from duty and had returned to the wagon. So Ike posted one of the men who was next on guard to tell Stubb what to expect, and to be sure to tell it to him scary.

A brief description of Stubb necessarily intrudes, though this nickname describes the man. Extremely short in stature, he was inclined to be fleshy. In fact, a rear view of Stubb looked as though someone had hollowed out a place to set his head between his ample shoulders. But a front view revealed a face like a full moon. In disposition he was very amiable. His laugh was enough to drive away 'the worst case of the blues. It bubbled up from some inward source and seemed perennial. His worst fault was his barroom astronomy. If there was any one thing that he shone in, it was rustling coffin varnish during the early prohibition days along the Kansas border. His patronage was limited only by his income, coupled with what credit he enjoyed.

Once, about midnight, he tried to arouse a drug clerk who slept in the store, and as he had worked this racket before, he coppered the play to repeat. So he tapped gently on the window at the rear where the clerk slept, calling him by name. This he repeated any number of times. Finally, he threatened to have a fit; even this did not work to his advantage. Then he pretended to be very angry, but there was no response. After fifteen minutes had been fruitlessly spent, he went back to the window, tapped on it once more, saying, "Lon, lie still, you little son-of-a-sheep-thief,'' which may not be what he said, and walked away. A party who had forgotten his name was once inquiring for him, describing him thus, ''He's a little short, fat fellow, sits around the Maverick Hotel, talks cattle talk, and punishes a power of whiskey.''

So before Stubb had even time to unsaddle his horse, he was approached to know the history of these two trails.

''Well,'' said Stubb somewhat hesitatingly, ''I never like to refer to it. You see, I killed a man the day that right-hand trail was made; I'll tell you about it some other time.''

''But why not now?'' said Lucy, his curiosity aroused, as keen as a woman's.

''Some other day,'' said Stubb. ''But did you notice those three graves on the last ridge of sand hills to the right as we came out of the Cimarron bottoms yesterday? You did? Their tenants were killed over that trail; you see now why I hate to refer to it, don't you? I was afraid to go back to Texas for three years afterward.''

''But why not tell me?'' said the young man.

''Oh,'' said Stubb, as he knelt down to put a hobble on his horse, ''it would injure my reputation as a peaceable citizen, and I don't mind telling you that I expect to marry soon.''

Having worked up the proper interest in his listener, besides exacting a promise that he would not repeat the story where it might do injury to him, he dragged his saddle up to the campfire. Making a comfortable seat with it, he riveted his gaze on the fire, and with a splendid *sang-froid* reluctantly told the history of the double trail.

"You see," began Stubb, "the Chisholm route had been used more or less for ten years. This right-hand trail was made in '73. I bossed that year from Van Zandt County, for old Andy Erath, who, by the way, was a dead square cowman with not a hidebound idea in his make-up. Son, it was a pleasure to know old Andy. You can tell he was a good man, for if he ever got a drink too much, though he would never mention her otherwise, he always praised his wife. I've been with him up beyond the Yellowstone, two thousand miles from home, and you always knew when the old man was primed. He would praise his wife, and would call on us boys to confirm the fact that Mary, his wife, was a good woman.

"That year we had the better of twenty-nine hundred head, all steer cattle, threes and up, a likely bunch, better than these we are shadowing now. You see, my people are not driving this year, which is the reason that I am making a common hand with Inks. If I was to lay off a season, or go to the seacoast, I might forget the way. In those days I always hired my own men. The year that this right-hand trail was made, I had an outfit of men who would rather fight than eat; in fact, I selected them on account of their special fitness in the use of firearms. Why, Inks here couldn't have cooked for my outfit that season, let alone rode. There was no particular incident worth mentioning till we struck Red River, where we overtook five or six herds that were laying over on account of a freshet in the river. I wouldn't have a man those days who was not as good in the water as out. When I rode up to the river, one or two of my men were with me. It looked red and muddy and rolled just a trifle, but I ordered one of the boys to hit it on his horse, to see what it was like. Well, he never wet the seat of his saddle going or coming, though his horse was in swimming water good sixty yards. All the other bosses rode up, and each one examined his peg to see if the rise was falling. One fellow named Bob Brown, boss man for John Blocker, asked me what I thought about the crossing. I said to him, 'If this ferryman can cross our wagon for me, and you fellows will open out a little and let me in, I'll show you all a crossing, and it'll be no miracle either.'

"Well, the ferryman said he'd set the wagon over, so the men went back to bring up the herd. They were delayed some little time, changing to their swimming horses. It was nearly an hour before the herd came up, the others opening out, so as to give us a clear field, in case of a mill or balk. I never had to give an order; my boys knew just what to do. Why, there's men in this outfit right now that couldn't have greased my wagon that year.

"Well, the men on the points brought the herd to the water with a good head on, and before the leaders knew it, they were halfway across the channel, swimming like fish. The swing men fed them in, free and plenty. Most of my outfit took to the water, and kept the cattle from drifting downstream. The boys from the other herds—good men, too—kept shooting them into the water, and inside fifteen minutes' time we were in the big Injun Territory. After crossing the saddle stock and the wagon, I swam my horse back to the Texas side. I wanted to eat dinner with Blocker's man, just to see how they fed. Might want to work for him sometime, you see. I pretended that I'd help him over if he wanted to cross, but he said his dogies could never breast that water. I remarked to him at dinner, 'You're feeding a mite better this year, ain't you?' 'Not that I can notice,' he replied, as the cook handed him a tin plate heaping with navy beans, 'and I'm eating rather regular with the wagon, too.' I killed time around for a while, and then we rode down to the river together. The cattle had tramped out his peg, so after setting a new one, and powwowing around, I told him good-by and said to him, 'Bob, old man, when I hit Dodge, I'll take a drink and think of you back here on the trail, and regret that you are not with me, so as to make it two-handed.' We said our 'so-longs' to each other, and I gave the gray his head and he took the water like a duck. He could outswim any horse I ever saw, but I drownded him in the Washita two weeks later. Yes, tangled his feet in some vines in a sunken treetop, and the poor fellow's light went out. My own candle came near being snuffed. I never felt so bad over a little thing since I burned my new red top-boots when I was a kid, as in drownding that horse.

"There was nothing else worth mentioning until we struck the Cimarron back here, where we overtook a herd of Chisholm's that had come in from the east. They had crossed through the Arbuckle Mountains—came in over the old Whiskey Trail. Here was another herd waterbound, and the boss man was as important as a hen with one chicken. He told me that the river wouldn't be fordable for a week; wanted me to fall back at least five miles; wanted all this river bottom for his cattle; said he didn't need any help to cross his herd, though he thanked me for the offer with an air of contempt. I informed him that our cattle were sold for delivery on the North Platte, and that we wanted to go through on time. I assured him if he would drop his cattle a mile down the river, it would give us plenty of room. I told him plainly that our cattle, horses, and men could all swim, and that we never let a little thing like swimming water stop us.

"No! No! he couldn't do that; we might as well fall back and take our turn. 'Oh, well,' said I, 'if you want to act contrary about it, I'll go up to the Kingfisher crossing, only three miles above here. I've almost got time to cross yet this evening.'

"Then he wilted and inquired, 'Do you think I can cross if it swims them any?'

" 'I'm not doing your thinking, sir,' I answered, 'but I'll bring up eight or nine good men and help you rather than make a six-mile elbow.' I said this with some spirit and gave him a mean look.

" 'All right,' said he, 'bring up your boys, say eight o'clock, and we will try the ford. Let me add right here,' he continued, 'and I'm a stranger to you, young man, but my outfit don't take anybody's slack, and as I am older than you, let me give you this little bit of advice: when you bring your men here in the morning, don't let them whirl too big a loop, or drag their ropes looking for trouble, for I've got fellows with me that don't turn out of the trail for anybody.'

"'All right, sir,' I said. 'Really, I'm glad to hear that you have some good men, still I'm pained to find them on the wrong side of the river for travelers. But I'll be here in the morning,' I called back as I rode away. So telling my boys that we were likely to have some fun in the morning, and what to expect, I gave it no further attention. When we were catching up our horses next morning for the day, I ordered two of my lads on herd, which was a surprise to them, as they were both handy with a gun. I explained it to them all—that we wished to avoid trouble, but if it came up unavoidable, to overlook no bets—to copper every play as it fell.

"We got to the river too early to suit Chisholm's boss man. He seemed to think that his cattle would take the water better about ten o'clock. To kill time my boys rode across and back several times to see what the water was like. 'Well, anyone that would let as little swimming water as that stop them must be a heap sight sorry outfit,' remarked one-eyed Jim Reed, as he rode out of the river, dismounting to set his saddle forward and tighten his clinches, not noticing that this foreman heard him. I rode around and gave him a look, and he looked up at me and muttered, 'Scuse me, boss, I plumb forgot!' Then I rode back and apologized to this boss man, 'Don't pay any attention to my boys; they are just showing off, and are a trifle windy this morning.'

"'That's all right,' he retorted, 'but don't forget what I told you yesterday, and let it be enough said.'

"'Well, let's put the cattle in,' I urged, seeing that

he was getting hot under the collar. 'We're burning daylight, pardner.'

" 'Well, I'm going to cross my wagon first,' said he.

" 'That's a good idea,' I answered. 'Bring her up.' Their cook seemed to have a little sense, for he brought up his wagon in good shape. We tied some guy ropes to the upper side, and taking long ropes from the end of the tongue to the pommels of our saddles, the ease with which we set that commissary over didn't trouble anyone but the boss man, whose orders were not very distinct from the distance between banks. It was a good hour then before he would bring up his cattle. The main trouble seemed to be to devise means to keep their guns and cartridges dry, as though that was more important than getting the whole herd of nearly thirty-five hundred cattle over. We gave them a clean cloth until they needed us, but as they came up we divided out and were ready to give the lead a good push. If a cow changed his mind about taking a swim that morning, he changed it right back and took it. For in less than twenty minutes' time they were all over, much to the surprise of the boss and his men; besides, their weapons were quite dry; just the splash had wet them.

"I told the boss that we would not need any help to cross ours, but to keep well out of our way, as we would try and cross by noon, which ought to give him a good five-mile start. Well, we crossed and nooned, lying around on purpose to give them a good lead, and when we hit the trail back in these sand hills, there he was, not a mile ahead, and you can see there was no chance to get around. I intended to take the Dodge Trail, from this creek where we are now, but there we were, blocked in! I was getting a trifle wolfish over the way they were acting, so I rode forward to see what the trouble was.

" 'Oh, I'm in no hurry. You're driving too fast. This is your first trip, isn't it?' he inquired, as he felt a pair of checked pants drying on the wagon wheel.

" 'Don't you let any idea like that disturb your Christian spirit, old man,' I replied with some resentment. 'But if you think I am driving too fast, you might suggest some creek where I could delude myself with the idea, for a week or so, that it was not fordable.'

"Assuming an air of superiority he observed, 'You seem to have forgot what I said to you yesterday.'

" 'No, I haven't,' I answered, 'but are you going to stay all night here?'

" 'I certainly am, if that's any satisfaction to you,' he answered.

"I got off my horse and asked him for a match, though I had plenty in my pocket, to light a cigarette which I had rolled during the conversation. I had no gun on, having left mine in our wagon, but fancied I'd stir him up and see how bad he really was. I thought it best to stroke him with and against the fur, try and keep on neutral ground, so I said—

" 'You ain't figuring none that in case of a run tonight we're a trifle close together for cow herds. Besides, my men on a guard last night heard gray wolves in these sand hills. They are liable to show up tonight. Didn't I notice some young calves among your cattle this morning? Young calves, you know, make larruping fine eating for grays.'

" 'Now, look here, Shorty,' he said in a patronizing tone, as though he might let a little of his superior cow sense shine in on my darkened intellect, 'I haven't asked you to crowd up here on me. You are perfectly at liberty to drop back to your heart's content. If wolves bother us tonight, you stay in your blankets snug and warm, and pleasant dreams of old sweethearts on the Trinity to you. We won't need you. We'll try and worry along without you.'

"Two or three of his men laughed gruffly at these remarks, and threw leer-eyed looks at me. I asked one who seemed bad, what caliber his gun was. 'Forty-five ha'r trigger,' he answered. I nosed around over their plunder on purpose. They had things drying around like Bannock squaws jerking venison.

"When I got on my horse, I said to the boss, 'I want to pass your outfit in the morning, as you are in no hurry and I am.'

" 'That will depend,' said he.

" 'Depend on what?' I asked.

" 'Depend on whether we are willing to let you,' he snarled.

"I gave him as mean a look as I could command and said tauntingly, 'Now, look here, old girl, there's no occasion for you to tear your clothes with me this way. Besides, I sometimes get on the prod myself, and when I do, I don't bar no man, Jew nor Gentile, horse, mare or gelding. You may think different, but I'm not afraid of any man in your outfit, from the gimlet to the big auger. I've tried to treat you white, but I see I've failed. Now I want to give it out to you straight and cold, that

I'll pass you tomorrow, or mix two herds trying. Think it over tonight and nominate your choice—be a gentleman or a hog. Let your own sweet will determine which.'

"I rode away in a walk, to give them a chance to say anything they wanted to, but there were no further remarks. My men were all hopping mad when I told them, but I promised them that tomorrow we would fix them plenty or use up our supply of cartridges if necessary. We dropped back a mile off the trail and camped for the night. Early the next morning I sent one of my boys out on the highest sand dune to Injun around and see what they were doing. After being gone for an hour he came back and said they had thrown their cattle off the bed-ground up the trail, and were pottering around like as they aimed to move. Breakfast over, I sent him back again to make sure, for I wanted yet to avoid trouble if they didn't draw it on. It was another hour before he gave us the signal to come on. We were nicely strung out where you saw those graves on that last ridge of sand hills, when there they were about a mile ahead of us, moseying along. This side of Chapman's, the Indian trader's store, the old route turns to the right and follows up this blackjack ridge. We kept up close, and just as soon as they turned in to the right—the only trail there was then—we threw off the course and came straight ahead, cross-country style, same route we came over today, except there was no trail there; we had to make a new one.

"Now they watched us a-plenty, but it seemed they couldn't make out our game. When we pulled up even with them, half a mile apart, they tumbled that my bluff of the day before was due to take effect without further notice. Then they began to circle and ride around, and one fellow went back, only hitting the high places, to their wagon and saddle horses, and they were brought up on a trot. We were by this time three quarters of a mile apart, when the boss of their outfit was noticed riding out toward us. Calling one of my men, I rode out and met him halfway. 'Young man, do you know just what you are trying to do?' he asked.

" 'I think I do. You and myself as cowmen don't pace in the same class, as you will see, if you will only watch the smoke of our tepee. Watch us close, and I'll pass you between here and the next water.'

" 'We will see you in hell first!' he said, as he whirled his horse and galloped back to his men. The race was on in a brisk walk. His wagon, we noticed, cut in between the herds, until it reached the lead of his cattle, when it halted suddenly, and we noticed that they were cutting off a dry cowskin that swung under the wagon. At the same time two of his men cut out a wild steer, and as he ran near their wagon one of them roped and the other heeled him. It was neatly done. I called Big Dick, my boss roper, and told him what I suspected—that they were going to try and stampede us with a dry cowskin tied to that steer's tail they had down. As they let him up, it was clear I had called the turn, as they headed him for our herd, the flint thumping at his heels. Dick rode out in a lope, and I signaled for my crowd to come on and we would back Dick's play. As we rode out together, I said to my boys, 'The stuff's off, fellows! Shoot, and shoot to hurt!'

"It seemed their whole outfit was driving that one steer, and turning the others loose to graze. Dick never changed the course of that steer, but let him head for ours, and as they met and passed, he turned his horse and rode onto him as though he was a post driven in the ground. Whirling a loop big enough to take in a yoke of oxen, he dropped it over his off fore shoulder, took up his slack rope, and when that steer went to the end of the rope, he was thrown in the air and came down on his head with a broken neck. Dick shook the rope off the dead steer's forelegs without dismounting, and was just beginning to coil his rope when those varmints made a dash at him, shooting and yelling.

"That called for a counterplay on our part, except our aim was low, for if we didn't get a man, we were sure to leave one afoot. Just for a minute the air was full of smoke. Two horses on our side went down before you could say 'Jack Robinson,' but the men were unhurt, and soon flattened themselves on the ground Indian fashion, and burnt the grass in a half-circle in front of them. When everybody had emptied his gun, each outfit broke back to its wagon to reload. Two of my men came back afoot, each claiming that he had got his man all right, all right. We were no men shy, which was lucky. Filling our guns with cartridges out of our belts, we rode out to reconnoiter and try and get the boys' saddles.

"The first swell of the ground showed us the field. There was the dead steer, and five or six horses scattered around likewise, but the grass was too high to show the men that we felt were there. As the opposition was keeping close to their wagon, we rode up to the scene of carnage. While some of the boys were getting the saddles off the dead horses, we found three men taking their last nap in the grass. I recognized them as the boss man, the fellow with the ha'r-trigger gun, and a fool kid that had two guns on him when we were crossing their cattle the day before. One gun wasn't plenty to do the fighting he was hankering for; he had about as much use for two guns as a toad has for a stinger.

"The boys got the saddles off the dead horses, and went flying back to our men afoot, and then rejoined us. The fight seemed over, or there was some hitch in the program, for we could see them hovering near their wagon, tearing up white biled shirts out of a trunk and bandaging up arms and legs, that they hadn't figured on any. Our herd had been overlooked during the scrimmage, and had scattered so that I had to send one man and the horse wrangler to round them in. We had ten men left, and it was beginning to look as though hostilities had ceased by mutual consent. You can see, son, we didn't bring it on. We turned over the dead steer, and he proved to be a stray; at least he hadn't their road brand on. One-eyed Jim said the ranch brand belonged in San Saba County; he knew it well, the X Bar 2. Well, it wasn't long until our men afoot got a remount and only two horses shy on the first round. We could stand another on the same terms in case they attacked us. We rode out on a little hill about a quarter mile from their wagon, scattering out so as not to give them a pot shot, in case they wanted to renew the unpleasantness.

"When they saw us there, one fellow started toward

us, waving his handkerchief. We began speculating which one it was, but soon made him out to be the cook; his occupation kept him out of the first round. When he came within a hundred yards, I rode out and met him. He offered me his hand and said, 'We are in a bad fix. Two of our crowd have bad flesh wounds. Do you suppose we could get any whiskey back at this Indian trader's store?'

" 'If there is any man in this territory can get any I can if they have it,' I told him. 'Besides, if your layout has had all the satisfaction fighting they want, we'll turn to and give you a lift. It seems like you all have some dead men over back here. They will have to be planted. So if your outfit feel as though you had your bellyful of fighting for the present, consider us at your service. You're the cook, ain't you?'

" 'Yes, sir,' he answered. 'Are all three dead?' he then inquired.

" 'Dead as heck,' I told him.

" 'Well, we are certainly in a bad box,' said he meditatingly. 'But won't you all ride over to our wagon with me? I think our fellows are pacified for the present.'

"I motioned to our crowd, and we all rode over to their wagon with him. There wasn't a gun in sight. The ragged edge of despair don't describe them. I made them a little talk; told them that their boss had cashed in, back over the hill; also if there was any *segundo* in their outfit, the position of big augur was open to him, and we were at his service.

"There wasn't a man among them that had any sense left but the cook. He told me to take charge of the killed, and if I could rustle a little whiskey to do so. So I told the cook to empty out his wagon, and we would take the dead ones back, make boxes for them, and bury them at the store. Then I sent three of my men back to the store to have the boxes ready and dig the graves. Before these three rode away, I said, aside to Jim, who was one of them, 'Don't bother about any whiskey; branch water is plenty nourishing for the wounded. It would be a sin and shame to waste good liquor on paltry like them.'

"The balance of us went over to the field of carnage and stripped the saddles off their dead horses, and arranged the departed in a row, covering them with saddle blankets, pending the planting act. I sent part of my boys with our wagon to look after our own cattle for the day. It took us all the afternoon to clean up a minute's work in the morning.

"I never like to refer to it. Fact was, all the boys felt gloomy for weeks, but there was no avoiding it. Two months later, we met old man Andy, way up at Fort Laramie on the North Platte. He was tickled to death to meet us all. The herd had come through in fine condition. We never told him anything about this until the cattle were delivered, and we were celebrating the success of that drive at a nearby town.

"Big Dick told him about this incident, and the old man feeling his oats, as he leaned with his back against the bar, said to us with a noticeable degree of pride, 'Lads, I'm proud of every one of you. Men who will fight to protect my interests have my purse at their command. This year's drive has been a success. Next year we will drive twice as many. I want every rascal of you to work for me. You all know how I mount, feed, and pay my men, and as long as my name is Erath and I own a cow, you can count on a job with me.' "

"But why did you take them back to the sand hills to bury them?" cut in Lucy.

"Oh, that was Big Dick's idea. He thought the sand would dig easier, and laziness guided every act of his life. That was five years ago, son, that this lower trail was made, and for the reasons I have just given you. No, I can't tell you any more personal experiences tonight; I'm too sleepy."

In a Spur of the County

told by
Conejo

Sergeant Smoky and four other Rangers had been out on special duty, and now we had halted after an all night's ride looking for shade and water, the latter especially. We had two prisoners—horse thieves—some extra saddle stock, and three pack mules.

We put the prisoners to roasting the ribs of an antelope that Cushion-Foot had shot and making themselves useful in general. One man guarded them at their work, while all the others attended to the hobbling and other camp duties.

It proved to be a delightful camp. We aimed to stay until sunset, the days being sultry and hot. Our appetites were equal to the breakfast, and it was a good one.

"To do justice to an occasion like this," said Smoky as he squatted down with about four ribs in his hand, "a man by rights ought to have at least three fingers of good liquor under his belt. But then we can't have all the luxuries of life in the far West; sure to be something lacking."

"I never hear a man hanker for liquor," said Conejo, as he poured out a tin cup of coffee, "but I think of an incident my father used to tell us boys at home. He was sheriff in Kentucky before we moved to Texas. Was sheriff in the same county for twelve years. Counties are very irregular back in the old states. Some look like a Mexican brand. One of the rankest, rabid political admirers my father had lived away out in a spur of this county. He lived a good thirty miles from the county seat. Didn't come to town over twice a year, but he always stopped, generally overnight, at our house. My father wouldn't have it any other way. Talk about thieves being chummy—why, these two we have here couldn't hold a candle to that man and my father. I can see them parting just as distinctly as though it was yesterday. He would always abuse my father for not coming to see him. 'Sam,' he would say—my father's name was Sam—'Sam, why on earth is it that you never come to see me? I've heard of you within ten miles of my plantation, and you have never shown your face to us once. Do you think we can't entertain you? Why, Sam, I've known you since you weren't big enough to lead a hound dog. I've known you since you weren't knee-high to a grasshopper.'

" 'Let me have a word,' my father would put in, for he was very mild in speaking; 'let me have a word, Joe. I hope you don't think for a moment that I wouldn't like to visit you, now do you?'

" 'No, I don't think so, Sam, but you don't come. That's why I'm complaining. You never have come in the whole ten years you've been sheriff, and you know that we have voted for you to a man, in our neck of the woods.'

My father felt this last remark, though I think he never realized its gravity before, but he took him by one hand, and laying the other on his shoulder said, 'Joe, if I have slighted you in the past, I'm glad you have called my attention to it. Now, let me tell you the first time that my business takes me within ten miles of your place I'll make it a point to reach your house and stay all night, and longer if I can.'

" 'That's all I ask, Sam,' was his only reply.

"Now I've learned lots of the ways of the world since then. I've seen people pleasant to each other, and behind their backs the tune changed. But I want to say to you fellows that those two old boys were not throwing off on each other—not a little bit. They meant every word and meant it deep.

"It was months afterwards, and Father had been gone for a week when he came home. He told us about his visit to Joe Evans. It was wintertime, and Mother and us boys were sitting around the old fireplace in the evening.

" 'I never saw him so embarrassed before in my life,' said Father. 'I did ride out of my way, but I was glad of the chance. Men like Joe Evans are getting scarce.' He nodded to us boys. 'It was nearly dark when I rode up to his gate. He recognized me and came down to the gate to meet me. "Howdy, Sam," was all he said. There was a troubled expression in his face, though he looked well enough, but he simply couldn't look me in the face. Just kept his eye on the ground. He motioned for a nigger boy and said to him, "Take his horse." He started to lead the way up the path, when I stopped him. "Look here, Joe," I said to him. "Now, if there's anything wrong, anything likely to happen in the family, I can just as well drop back on the pike and stay all night with some of the neighbors. You know I'm acquainted all around here."

" 'He turned in the path, and there was the most painful look in his face I ever saw as he spoke, "Hell, no, Sam, there's nothing wrong. We've got plenty to eat, plenty of beds, no end of horse feed, but by G——, Sam, there isn't a drop of whiskey on the place!" '

"You see it was hoss and *caballo,* and Joe seemed to think the hoss on him was an unpardonable offense. Salt? You'll find it in an empty one-spoon baking-powder can over there. In those panniers that belong to that big sorrel mule. Look at Mexico over there burying his fangs in the venison, will you?"

Judge Bean in Court

told by
Sergeant Smoky

After breakfast was over we smoked and yarned. It would be two-hour guards for the day, keeping an eye on the prisoners and stock, only one man required; so we would all get plenty of sleep. Conejo had the first guard after breakfast.

"I remember once," said Sergeant Smoky, as he crushed a pipe of twist with the heel of his hand, "we were camped out on the 'Sunset' railway. I was a corporal at the time. There came a message one day to our captain, to send a man up west on that line to take charge of a murderer. The result was, I was sent by the first train to this point. When I arrived I found that an Irishman had killed a Chinaman. It was on the railroad, at a bridge-construction camp, that the fracas took place. There was something like a hundred employees at the camp, and they ran their own boarding tent. They had a Chinese cook at this camp; in fact, quite a number of Chinese were employed at common labor on the road.

"Some cavalryman, it was thought, in passing up and down from Fort Stockton to points on the river, had lost his saber, and one of this bridge gang had found it. When it was brought into camp no one would have the old corn cutter; but this Irishman took a shine to it, having once been a soldier himself. The result was, it was presented to him. He ground it up like a machete, and took great pride in giving exhibitions with it. He was an old man now, the storekeeper for the iron supplies, a kind of trusty job. The old saber renewed his youth to a certain extent, for he used it in self-defense shortly afterwards.

"This Erin-go-bragh—his name was McKay, I think—was in the habit now and then of stealing a pie from the cook, and taking it into his own tent and eating it there. The Chink kept missing his pies, and got a helper to spy out the offender. The result was they caught the old man red-handed in the act. The Chink armed himself with the biggest butcher knife he had and went on the warpath. He found the old fellow sitting in his storeroom contentedly eating the pie. The old man had his eyes on the cook, and saw the knife just in time to jump behind some kegs of nuts and bolts. The Chink followed him with murder in his eye, and as the old man ran out of the tent he picked up the old saber. Once clear of the tent he turned and faced him, made only one pass, and cut his head off as though he were beheading a chicken. They hadn't yet buried the Chinaman when I got there. I'm willing to testify it was an artistic job.

"They turned the old man over to me, and I took him down to the next station, where an old alcalde lived—Roy Bean by name. This old judge was known as 'Law west of the Pecos,' as he generally construed the law to suit his own opinion of the offense. He wasn't even strong on testimony. He was a ranchman at this time, so when I presented my prisoner he only said, 'Killed a Chinese, did he? Well, I ain't got time to try the case today. Cattle suffering for water, and three windmills out of repair. Bring him back in the morning.' I took the old man back to the hotel, and we had a jolly good time together that day. I never put a string on him, only locked the door, but we slept together. The next morning I took him before the alcalde. Bean held court in an outhouse, the prisoner seated on a bale of flint hides. Bean was not only judge but prosecutor, as well as counsel for the defense.

" 'Killed a Chinaman, did you?'

" 'I did, yer Honor,' was the prisoner's reply.

"I suggested to the court that the prisoner be informed of his rights, that he need not plead guilty unless he so desired.

" 'That makes no difference here,' said the court. 'Gentlemen, I'm busy this morning. I've got to raise the piping out of a two-hundred-foot well today—something the matter with the valve at the bottom. I'll just glance over the law a moment.'

"He rummaged over a book or two for a few moments and then said, 'Here, I reckon this is near enough. I find in the revised statute before me, in the killing of a nigger the offending party was fined five dollars. A Chinaman ought to be half as good as a nigger. Stand up and receive your sentence. What's your name?'

" 'Jerry McKay, yer Honor.'

"Just then the court noticed one of the vaqueros belonging to the ranch standing in the door, hat in hand, and he called to him in Spanish, 'Have my horse ready, I'll be through here in just a minute.'

" 'McKay,' said the court as he gave him a withering look, 'I'll fine you two dollars and a half and costs. Officer, take charge of the prisoner until it's paid!' It took about ten dollars to cover everything, which I paid, McKay returning it when he reached his camp. Whoever named that alcalde 'Law west of the Pecos' knew his man."

A Skirmish on the Head of the Arroyo Colorado

told by
Ramrod

Ramrod was on guard, but he was so hungry himself that he was good enough to let the prisoners eat at the same time, although he kept them at a respectable distance. He was old in the Ranger service, and had gotten his name under a baptism of fire. He was watching a pass once for smugglers at a point called Emigrant Gap. This was long before he had come to the present company. At length the man he was waiting for came along. Ramrod went after him at close quarters, but the fellow was game and drew his gun. When the smoke cleared away, Ramrod had brought down his horse and winged his man right and left. The smuggler was not far behind on the shoot, for Ramrod's coat and hat showed he was calling for him. The captain was joshing the prisoner about his poor shooting when Ramrod brought him into camp and they were dressing his wounds. "Well," said the fellow, "I tried to hard enough, but I couldn't find him. He's built like a ramrod."

"I'll bet a twist of dog," said Ramrod, "that prisoner with the black whiskers sabes English. Did you notice him paying strict attention to Smoky's little talk? He reminds me of a fellow that crouched behind his horse at the fight we had on the head of the Arroyo Colorado and plugged me in the shoulder. What, you never heard of it? That's so, Cushion hasn't been with us but a few months. Well, it was in '82, down on the river, about fifty miles northwest of Brownsville. Word came in one day that a big band of horse thieves were sweeping the country of every horse they could gather. There was a number of the old Cortina's gang known to be still on the rustle. When this report came, it found eleven men in camp. We lost little time saddling up, only taking five days' rations with us, for they were certain to recross the river before that time in case we failed to intercept them. Every Mexican in the country was terrorized. All they could tell us was that there was plenty of ladrones and lots of horses, *muchos* being the qualifying word as to the number of either.

"It was night before we came to their trail, and to our surprise they were heading inland, to the north. They must have had a contract to supply the Mexican army with cavalry horses. They were simply sweeping the country, taking nothing but gentle stock. These they bucked in strings, and led. That made easy trailing, as each string left a distinct trail. The moon was splendid that night, and we trailed as easily as though it had been day. We didn't halt all night long on either trail, pegging along at a steady gait that would carry us inland some distance before morning. Our scouts aroused every ranch within miles that we passed on the way, only to have reports exaggerated as usual. One thing we did learn that night, and that was that the robbers were led by a white man. He was described in the superlatives that the Spanish language possesses abundantly; everything from the horse he rode to the solid braid on his sombrero was described in the same strain. But that kind of prize was the kind we were looking for.

"On the head of the Arroyo Colorado there is a broken country interspersed with glades and large openings. We felt very sure that the robbers would make camp somewhere in that country. When day broke, the freshness of the trail surprised and pleased us. They couldn't be far away. Before an hour passed, we noticed a smoke cloud hanging low in the morning air about a mile ahead. We dismounted and securely tied our horses and pack stock. Every man took all the cartridges he could use, and was itching for the chance to use them. We left the trail, and to conceal ourselves took to the brush or dry arroyos as a protection against alarming the quarry. They were a quarter of a mile off when we first sighted them. We began to think the reports were right, for there seemed no end of horses, and at least twenty-five men. By dropping back we could gain one of those dry arroyos which would bring us within one hundred yards of their camp. A young fellow by the name of Rusou, a crack shot, was acting captain in the absence of our officers. As we backed into the arroyo he said to us, 'If there's a white man there, leave him to me.' We were all satisfied that he would be cared for properly at Rusou's hands, and silence gave consent.

"Opposite the camp we wormed out of the arroyo like a skirmish line, hugging the ground for the one remaining little knoll between the robbers and ourselves. I was within a few feet of Rusou as we sighted the camp about seventy-five yards distant. We were trying to make out a man that was asleep; at least he had his hat over his face, lying on a blanket with his head in a saddle. We concluded he was a white man, if there was one. Our survey of their camp was cut short by two shots fired at us by two pickets of theirs posted to our left about one hundred yards. No one was hit, but the sleeping man jumped to his feet with a six-shooter in each hand. I heard Rusou say to himself, 'You're too late, my friend.' His carbine spoke, and the fellow fell forward, firing both guns into the ground at his feet as he went down.

"Then the stuff was off and she opened up in earnest. They fought all right. I was on my knee pumping lead for dear life, and as I threw my carbine down to refill the magazine, a bullet struck it in the heel of the magazine with sufficient force to knock me backward. I thought I was hit for an instant, but it passed away in a moment. When I tried to work the lever I saw that my carbine was ruined. I called to the boys to notice a fellow with black whiskers who was shooting from behind his horse. He would shoot over and under alternately. I thought he was shooting at me. I threw down my carbine and drew my six-shooter. Just then I got a plug in the shoulder, and things got dizzy and dark. It caught me an inch above the nipple, ranging upward—shooting from under, you see. But some of the boys must have noticed him, for he decorated the scene badly leaded, when it was over. I was unconscious for a few minutes, and when I came around the fight had ended.

"During the few brief moments that I was knocked out, our boys had closed in on them and mixed it with them at short range. The thieves took to such horses as they could lay their hands on, and one fellow went no farther. A six-shooter halted him at fifty yards. The boys rounded up over a hundred horses, each one with a fiber-grass halter on, besides killing over twenty wounded ones to put them out of their misery.

"It was a nasty fight. Two of our own boys were killed and three were wounded. But then you ought to have seen the other fellows; we took no prisoners that day. Nine men lay dead. Horses were dead and dying all around, and the wounded ones were crying in agony.

"This white man proved to be a typical dandy, a queer leader for such a gang. He was dressed in buckskin throughout, while his sombrero was as fine as money could buy. You can know it was a fine one, for it was sold for company prize money, and brought three hundred and fifty dollars. He had nearly four thousand dollars on his person and in his saddle. A belt which was found on him had eleven hundred in bills and six hundred in good old yellow gold. The silver in the saddle was mixed, Mexican and American about equally.

"He had as fine a gold watch in his pocket as you ever saw, while his firearms and saddle were beauties. He was a dandy all right, and a fine-looking man, over six feet tall, with swarthy complexion and hair like a raven's wing. He was too nice a man for the company he was in. We looked the 'Black Book' over afterward for any description of him. At that time there were over four thousand criminals and outlaws described in it, but there was no description that would fit him. For this reason we supposed that he must live far in the interior of Mexico.

"Our saddle stock was brought up, and our wounded were bandaged as best they could be. My wound was the worst, so they concluded to send me back. One of the boys went with me, and we made a fifty-mile ride before we got medical attention. While I was in the hospital I got my divvy of the prize money, something over four hundred dollars."

Viva los Timochis!

told by
Cushion-Foot

When Ramrod had finished his narrative, he was compelled to submit to a cross-examination at the hands of Cushion-Foot, for he delighted in a skirmish. All his questions being satisfactorily answered, Cushion-Foot drew up his saddle alongside of where Ramrod lay stretched on a blanket, and seated himself. This was a signal to the rest of us that he had a story, so we drew near, for he spoke so low that you must be near to hear him. His years on the frontier were rich in experience, though he seldom referred to them.

Addressing himself to Ramrod, he began. "You might live amongst these border Mexicans all your life and think you knew them; but every day you live you'll see new features about them. You can't calculate on them with any certainty. What they ought to do by any system of reasoning they never do. They will steal an article and then give it away. You've heard the expression 'robbing Peter to pay Paul.' Well, my brother played the role of Paul once himself. It was out in Arizona at a place called Las Palomas. He was a stripling of a boy, but could palaver Spanish in a manner that would make a Mexican ashamed of his ancestry. He was about eighteen at this time and was working in a store. One morning as he stepped outside the store, where he slept, he noticed quite a commotion over around the customhouse. He noticed that the town was full of strangers, as he crossed over toward the crowd. He was suddenly halted and searched by a group of strange men. Fortunately he had no arms on him, and his ability to talk to them, together with his boyish looks, ingratiated him in their favor, and they simply made him their prisoner. Just at that moment the alcalde rode up to the group about him, and was ordered to halt. He saw at a glance they were revolutionists, and whirling his mount attempted to escape, when one of them shot him from his horse. The young fellow then saw what he was into.

"They called themselves Timochis. They belonged in Mexico, and a year or so before they refused to pay taxes that the Mexican government levied on them, and rebelled. Their own government sent soldiers after them, resulting in about eight hundred soldiers being killed, when they dispersed into small bands, one of which was paying Las Palomas a social call that morning. Along the Rio Grande it is only a short step at best from revolution to robbery, and either calling has its variations.

"Well, they took my brother with them to act as spokesman in looting the town. The customhouse was a desired prize, and when my brother interpreted their desires to the collector, he consented to open the safe, as life had charms for him, even in Arizona. Uncle Sam's strongbox yielded up over a thousand dobes. They turned their attention to the few small stores of the town, looting them of the money and goods as they went. There was quite a large store kept by a Frenchman, who refused to open, when he realized that the Timochi was honoring the town with his presence. They put the boy in the front and ordered him to call on the Frenchman to open up. He said afterward that he put in a word for himself, telling him not to do any shooting through the door. After some persuasion the store was opened and proved to be quite a prize. Then they turned their attention to the store where the boy worked. He unlocked it and waved them in. He went into the cellar and brought up half a dozen bottles of imported French cognac, and invited the chief bandit and his followers to be good enough to join him. In the meantime they had piled up on the counters such things as they wanted. They made no money demand on him, the chief asking him to set a price on the things they were taking. He made a hasty inventory of the goods and gave the chief the figures, about one hundred and ten dollars. The chief opened a sack that they had taken from the customhouse and paid the bill with a flourish.

"The chief then said that he had a favor to ask: that my brother should cheer for the revolutionists, to identify him as a friend. That was easy, so he mounted the counter and gave three cheers of 'Viva los Timochis!' He got down off the counter, took the bandit by the arm, and led him to the rear, where with glasses in the air they drank to 'Viva los Timochis!' again. Then the chief and his men withdrew and recrossed the river. It was the best day's trade he had had in a long time. Now, here comes in the native. While the boy did everything from compulsion and policy, the native element looked upon him with suspicion. The owners of the store, knowing that this suspicion existed, advised him to leave, and he did."

Buffaloed by a Bear

told by
Orchard

When we had done justice to the supper, the twilight hours of the evening were spent in making camp snug for the night. Every horse or mule was either picketed or hobbled. Every man washed his saddle blankets, as the long, continuous ride had made them rancid with sweat. The night air was so dry and warm that they would even dry at night. There was the usual target practice and the never-ending cleaning of firearms. As night settled over the camp, everything was in order. The blankets were spread, and smoking and yarning occupied the time until sleep claimed us.

"Talking about the tight places," said Orchard, "in which a man often finds himself in this service, reminds me of a funny experience which I once had, out on the headwaters of the Brazos. I've smelt powder at short range, and I'm willing to admit there's nothing fascinating in it. But this time I got buffaloed by a bear.

"There are a great many brakes on the head of the Brazos, and in them grow cedar thickets. I forget now what the duty was that we were there on, but there were about twenty of us in the detachment at the time. One morning, shortly after daybreak, another lad and myself walked out to unhobble some extra horses which we had with us. The horses had strayed nearly a mile from camp, and when we found them they were cutting up as if they had been eating loco weed for a month. When we came up to them, we saw that they were scared. These horses couldn't talk, but they told us that just over the hill was something they were afraid of.

"We crept up the little hill, and there over in a draw was the cause of their fear—a big old lank cinnamon. He was feeding along, heading for a thicket of about ten acres. The lad who was with me stayed and watched him, while I hurried back, unhobbled the horses, and rushed them into camp. I hustled out every man, and they cinched their hulls on those horses rapidly. By the time we had reached the lad who had stayed to watch him, the bear had entered the thicket, still unalarmed. Some fool suggested the idea that we could drive him out in the open and rope him. The lay of the land would suggest such an idea, for beyond this motte of cedar lay an impenetrable thicket of over a hundred acres, which we thought he would head for if alarmed. There was a ridge of a divide between these cedar brakes, and if the bear should attempt to cross over, he would make a fine mark for a rope.

"Well, I always was handy with a rope, and the boys knew it, so I and three others who could twirl a rope were sent around on this divide, to rope him in case he came out. The others left their horses and made a half-circle drive through the grove, beating the brush and burning powder as though it didn't cost anything. We ropers up on the divide scattered out, hiding ourselves as much as we could in the broken places. We wanted to get him out in the clear in case he played nice. He must have been a sullen old fellow, for we were beginning to think they had missed him or he had holed, when he suddenly lumbered out directly opposite me and ambled away towards the big thicket.

"I was riding a cream-colored horse, and he was as good a one as ever was built on four pegs, except that he was nervous. He had never seen a bear, and when I gave him the rowel, he went after that bear like a cat after a mouse. The first sniff he caught of the bear, he whirled quicker than lightning, but I had made my cast, and the loop settled over Mr. Bear's shoulders, with one of his fore feet through it. I had tied the rope in a hard knot to the pommel, and the way my horse checked that bear was a caution. It must have made bruin mad. My horse snorted and spun round like a top, and in less time than it takes to tell it, there was a bear, a cream-colored horse, and a man sandwiched into a pile on the ground, and securely tied with a three-eighths-inch rope. The horse had lashed me into the saddle by winding the rope, and at the same time windlassed the bear in on top of us. The horse cried with fear as though he was being burnt to death, while the bear grinned and blew his breath in my face. The running noose in the rope had cut his wind so badly he could hardly offer much resistance. It was a good thing he had his wind cut, or he would have made me sorry I enlisted. I didn't know it at the time, but my six-shooter had fallen out of the holster, while the horse was lying on my carbine.

"The other three rode up and looked at me, and they all needed killing. Horse, bear, and man were so badly mixed up they dared not shoot. One laughed till he cried, another one was so near limp he looked like a ghost, while one finally found his senses and, dismounting, cut the rope in half a dozen places and untied the bundle. My horse floundered to his feet and ran off, but before the bear could free the noose, the boys got enough lead into him at close quarters to hold him down. The entire detachment came out of the thicket, and their hilarity knew no bounds. I was the only man in the crowd who didn't enjoy the bear chase. Right then I made a resolve that hereafter, when volunteers are called for to rope a bear, my accomplishments in that line will remain unmentioned by me. I'll eat my breakfast first, anyhow, and think it over carefully."

Buffaloed by a Bear

"Dogs and horses are very much alike about a bear," said one of the boys. "Take a dog that never saw a bear in his life, and let him get a sniff of one, and he'll get up his bristles like a javelina and tuck his tail and look about for good backing or a clear field to run."

A Little *Paseo* over into Mexico

told by
Long John

Long John showed symptoms that he had some yarn to relate, so we naturally remained silent to give him a chance, in case the spirit moved in him. Throwing a brand into the fire after lighting his cigarette, he stretched himself on the ground, and the expected happened.

"A few years ago, while rangering down the country," said he, "four of us had trailed some horse thieves down on the Rio Grande, when they gave us the slip by crossing over into Mexico. We knew the thieves were just across the river, so we hung around a few days, in the hope of catching them, for if they should recross into Texas they were our meat. Our plans were completely upset the next morning, by the arrival of twenty United States cavalrymen on the cold trail of four deserters. The fact that these deserters were five days ahead and had crossed into Mexico promptly on reaching the river, did not prevent this squad of soldiers from notifying both villages on each side of the river as to their fruitless errand. They couldn't follow their own any farther, and they managed to scare our quarry into hiding in the interior. We waited until the soldiers returned to the post, when we concluded we would take a little *paseo* over into Mexico on our own account.

"We called ourselves horse buyers. The government was paying like thirty dollars for deserters, and in case we run across them, we figured it would pay expenses to bring them out. These deserters were distinguishable whenever they went by the size of their horses; besides, they had two fine big American mules for packs. They were marked right for that country. Everything about them was *muy grande*. We were five days overtaking them, and then at a town one hundred and forty miles in the interior. They had celebrated their desertion the day previous to our arrival by getting drunk, and when the horse buyers arrived they were in jail. This last condition rather frustrated our plans for their capture, as we expected to kidnap them out. But now we had red tape authorities to deal with.

"We found the horses, mules, and accouterments in a corral. They would be no trouble to get, as the bill for their keep was the only concern of the corral keeper. Two of the boys who were in the party could palaver Spanish, so they concluded to visit the alcalde of the town, inquiring after horses in general and incidentally finding out when our deserters would be released. The alcalde received the boys with great politeness, for Americans were rare visitors in his town, and after giving them all the information available regarding horses, the subject innocently changed to the American prisoners in jail. The alcalde informed them that he was satisfied they were deserters, and not knowing just what to do with them, he had sent a courier that very morning to the governor for instructions in the matter. He estimated it would require at least ten days to receive the governor's reply. In the meantime, much as he regretted it, they would remain prisoners. Before parting, those two innocents permitted their host to open a bottle of wine as an evidence of the friendly feeling, and at the final leave-taking, they wasted enough politeness on each other to win a woman.

"When the boys returned to us other two, we were at our wit's end. We were getting disappointed too often. The result was that we made up our minds that rather than throw up, we would take those deserters out of jail and run the risk of getting away with them. We had everything in readiness an hour before nightfall. We explained, to the satisfaction of the Mexican hostler who had the stock in charge, that the owners of these animals were liable to be detained in jail possibly a month, and to avoid the expense of their keeping, we would settle the bill for our friends and take the stock with us. When the time came every horse was saddled and the mules packed and in readiness. We had even moved our own stock into the same corral, which was only a short distance from the jail.

"As night set in we approached the *cárcel*. The turnkey answered our questions very politely through a grated iron door, and to our request to speak with the prisoners, he regretted that they were being fed at that moment, and we would have to wait a few minutes. He unbolted the door, however, and offered to show us into a side room, an invitation we declined. Instead, we relieved him of his keys and made known our errand. When he discovered that we were armed and he was our prisoner, he was speechless with terror. It was short work to find the men we wanted and march them out, locking the gates behind us and taking jailer and keys with us. Once in the saddle, we bade the poor turnkey good-by and returned him his keys.

"We rode fast, but in less than a quarter of an hour there was a clanging of bells which convinced us that the alarm had been given. Our prisoners took kindly to the rescue and rode willingly, but we were careful to conceal our identity or motive. We felt certain there would be pursuit, if for no other purpose, to justify official authority. We felt easy, for we were well mounted, and if it came to a pinch, we would burn powder with them, one round at least.

"Before half an hour had passed, we were aware that we were pursued. We threw off the road at right angles and rode for an hour. Then, with the North Star for a guide, we put over fifty miles behind us before sunrise. It was impossible to secrete ourselves the next day, for we were compelled to have water for ourselves and stock. To conceal the fact that our friends were prisoners, we returned them their arms after throwing away their ammunition. We had to enter several ranches during the day to secure food and water, but made no particular effort to travel.

"About four o'clock we set out, and to our surprise, too, a number of horsemen followed us until nearly dark. Passing through a slight shelter, in which we were out of sight some little time, two of us dropped back and awaited our pursuers. As they came up within hailing distance, we ordered them to halt, which they declined by whirling their horses and burning the earth getting away. We threw a few rounds of lead after them, but they cut all desire for our acquaintance right there.

"We reached the river at a nearer point than the one at which we had entered, and crossed to the Texas side early the next morning. We missed a good ford by two miles and swam the river. At this ford was stationed a squad of regulars, and we turned our prizes over within an hour after crossing. We took a receipt for the men, stock, and equipments, and when we turned it over to our captain a week afterwards, we got the riot act read to us right. I noticed, however, the first time there was a division of prize money, one item was for the capture of four deserters."

"I don't reckon that captain had any scruples about taking his share of the prize money, did he?" inquired Gotch.

"No, I never knew anything like that to happen since I've been in the Ranger service."

A Comanche Fight in the Tallow Cache Hills

told by
Dad Root

Amongst Dad's other accomplishments was his unfailing readiness to tell of his experiences with the Texas Rangers. So after he had looked over the camp in general, he joined the group of lounging smokers and told us of an Indian fight in which he had participated.

"I can't imagine how this comes to be called Comanche Ford," said Dad. "Now the Comanches crossed over into the Panhandle country annually for the purpose of killing buffalo. For diversion and pastime, they were always willing to add horse-stealing and the murdering of settlers as a variation. They used to come over in big bands to hunt, and when ready to go back to their reservation in the Indian Territory, they would send the squaws on ahead, while the bucks would split into small bands and steal all the good horses in sight.

"Our old company was ordered out on the border once, when the Comanches were known to be south of Red River killing buffalo. This meant that on their return it would be advisable to look out for your horses or they would be missing. In order to cover as much territory as possible, the company was cut in three detachments. Our squad had twenty men in it under a lieutenant. We were patrolling a country known as the Tallow Cache Hills, glades and blackjack cross timbers alternating. All kinds of rumors of Indian depredations were reaching us almost daily, yet so far we had failed to locate or see an Indian.

"One day at noon we packed up and were going to move our camp farther west, when a scout, who had gone on ahead, rushed back with the news that he had sighted a band of Indians with quite a herd of horses pushing north. We led our pack mules, and keeping the shelter of the timber started to cut them off in their course. When we first sighted them, they were just crossing a glade, and the last buck had just left the timber. He had in his mouth an arrow shaft, which he was turning between his teeth to remove the sap. All had guns. The first warning the Indians received of our presence was a shot made by one of the men at this rear Indian. He rolled off his horse like a stone, and the next morning when we came back over their trail, he had that unfinished arrow in a death grip between his teeth. That first shot let the cat out, and we went after them.

"We had two big piebald calico mules, and when we charged those Indians, those pack mules outran every saddle horse which we had, and dashing into their horse herd, scattered them like partridges. Nearly every buck was riding a stolen horse, and for some cause they couldn't get any speed out of them. We just rode all around them. There proved to be twenty-two Indians in the band, and one of them was a squaw. She was killed by accident.

"The chase had covered about two miles, when the horse she was riding fell from a shot by some of our crowd. The squaw recovered herself and came to her feet in time to see several carbines in the act of being leveled at her by our men. She instantly threw open the slight covering about her shoulders and revealed her sex. Someone called out not to shoot, that it was a squaw, and the carbines were lowered. As this squad passed on, she turned and ran for the protection of the nearest timber, and a second squad coming up and seeing the fleeing Indian, fired on her, killing her instantly. She had done the very thing she should not have done.

"It was a running fight from start to finish. We got the last one in the band about seven miles from the first one. The last one to fall was mounted on a fine horse, and if he had only ridden intelligently, he ought to have escaped. The funny thing about it was he was overtaken by the dullest, sleepiest horse in our command. The shooting and smell of powder must have put iron into him, for he died a hero. When this last Indian saw that he was going to be overtaken, his own horse being recently wounded, he hung on one side of the animal and returned the fire. At a range of ten yards he planted a bullet squarely in the leader's forehead, his own horse falling at the same instant. Those two horses fell dead so near that you could have tied their tails together. Our man was thrown so suddenly that he came to his feet dazed, his eyes filled with dirt. The Indian stood not twenty steps away and fired several shots at him. Our man, in his blindness, stood there and beat the air with his gun, expecting the Indian to rush on him every moment. Had the buck used his gun for a club, it might have been different, but as long as he kept shooting, his enemy was safe. Half a dozen of us, who were near enough to witness his final fight, dashed up, and the Indian fell riddled with bullets.

"We went into camp after the fight was over with two wounded men and a half dozen dead or disabled horses. Those of us who had mounts in good fix scoured back and gathered in our packs and all the Indian and stolen horses that were unwounded. It looked like a butchery, but our minds were greatly relieved on that point the next day, when we found among their effects over a dozen fresh, bloody scalps, mostly women and children. There's times and circumstances in this service that make the toughest of us gloomy."

"How long ago was that?" inquired Orchard.

"Quite a while ago," replied Dad. "I ought to be able to tell exactly. I was a youngster then. Well, I'll tell you; it was during the reconstruction days, when Davis was governor. Figure it out yourself."

El Lobo's Sweetheart

told by
Happy Jack

"Speaking of the disagreeable side of this Ranger service," said Happy Jack, "reminds me of an incident that took all the nerve out of everyone connected with it. When I first went into the service, there was a well-known horse thief and smuggler down the river, known as El Lobo. He operated on both sides of the Rio Grande, but generally stole his horses from the Texas side. He was a night owl. It was nothing for him to be seen at some ranch in the evening, and the next morning be met seventy-five or eighty miles distant. He was a good judge of horseflesh, and never stole any but the best. His market was well in the interior of Mexico, and he supplied it liberally. He was a typical dandy, and like a sailor had a wife in every port. That was his weak point, and there's where we attacked him.

"He had made all kinds of fun of this service, and we concluded to have him at any cost. Accordingly we located his women and worked on them. Mexican beauty is always overrated, but one of his conquests in that line came as near being the ideal for a rustic beauty as that nationality produces. This girl was about twenty, and lived with a questionable mother at a ranchito back from the river about thirty miles. In form and feature there was nothing lacking, while the smoldering fire of her black eyes would win saint or thief alike. Born in poverty and ignorance, she was a child of circumstance, and fell an easy victim to El Lobo, who lavished every attention upon her. There was no present too costly for him, and on his periodical visits he dazzled her with gifts. But infatuations of that class generally have an end, often a sad one.

"We had a half-blood in our company, who was used as a rival to El Lobo in gathering any information that might be afloat, and at the same time, when opportunity offered, in sowing the wormwood of jealousy. This was easy, for we collected every item in the form of presents he ever made her rival *señoritas*. When these forces were working, our half-blood pushed his claims for recognition. Our wages and prize money were at his disposal, and in time they won. The neglect shown her by El Lobo finally turned her against him, apparently, and she agreed to betray his whereabouts the first opportunity—on one condition. And that was, that if we succeeded in capturing him, we were to bring him before her, that she might, in his helplessness, taunt him for his perfidy towards her. We were willing to make any concession to get him, so this request was readily granted.

"The deserted condition of the ranchito where the girl lived was to our advantage as well as his. The few families that dwelt there had their flocks to look after, and the coming or going of a passer-by was scarcely noticed. Our man on his visits carefully concealed the fact that he was connected with this service, for El Lobo's lavish use of money made him friends wherever he went, and afforded him all the seclusion he needed.

"It was over a month before the wolf made his appearance, and we were informed of the fact. He stayed at an outside *pastor*'s camp, visiting the ranch only after dark. A corral was mentioned, where within a few days' time, at the farthest, he would pen a bunch of saddle horses. There had once been wells at this branding pen, but on their failing to furnish water continuously they had been abandoned. El Lobo had friends at his command to assist him in securing the best horses in the country. So accordingly we planned to pay our respects to him at these deserted wells.

"The second night of our watch, we were rewarded by having three men drive into these corrals about twenty saddle horses. They had barely time to tie their mounts outside and enter the pen, when four of us slipped in behind them and changed the program a trifle. El Lobo was one of the men. He was very polite and nice, but that didn't prevent us from ironing him securely, as we did his companions also.

"It was almost midnight when we reached the ranchito where the girl lived. We asked him if he had any friends at this ranch whom he wished to see. This he denied. When we informed him that by special request a lady wished to bid him farewell, he lost some of his bluster and bravado. We all dismounted, leaving one man outside with the other two prisoners, and entered a small yard where the girl lived. Our half-blood aroused her and called her out to meet her friend, El Lobo. The girl delayed us some minutes, and we apologized to him for the necessity of irons and our presence in meeting his *dulce corazón.* When the girl came out we were some distance from the jacal. There was just moonlight enough to make her look beautiful.

"As she advanced, she called him by some pet name in their language, when he answered her gruffly, accusing her of treachery, and turned his back upon her. She approached within a few feet, when it was noticeable that she was racked with emotion, and asked him if he had no kind word for her. Turning on her, he repeated the accusation of treachery, and applied a vile expression to her. That moment the girl flashed into a fiend, and throwing a shawl from her shoulders, revealed a pistol, firing it twice before a man could stop her. El Lobo sank in his tracks, and she begged us to let her trample his lifeless body. Later, when composed, she told us that we had not used her any more than she had used us, in bringing him helpless to her. As things turned out it looked that way.

"We lashed the dead thief on his horse and rode until daybreak, when we buried him. We could have gotten a big reward for him dead or alive, and we had the evidence of his death, but the manner in which we got it made it undesirable. El Lobo was missed, but the manner of his going was a secret of four men and a Mexican girl. The other two prisoners went over the road, and we even reported to them that he had attempted to strangle her, and we shot him to save her. Something had to be said."

Raneka Bill Hunter

told by
Mouse

They were singing over at one of the wagons across the draw, and after the song ended, Bradshaw asked, "What ever became of Raneka Bill Hunter?"

"Oh, he's drifting about," said Edwards. "Mouse here can tell you about him. They're old college chums."

"Raneka was working for the Bar B Q people last summer," said Mouse, "but was discharged for hanging a horse, or rather he discharged himself. It seems that someone took a fancy to a horse in his mount. The last man to buy into an outfit that way always gets all the bad horses for his string. As Raneka was a new man there, the result was that some excuse was given him to change, and they rung in a spoilt horse on him in changing. Being new that way, he wasn't on to the horses. The first time he tried to saddle this new horse he showed up bad. The horse trotted up to him when the rope fell on his neck, reared up nicely and playfully, and threw out his forefeet, stripping the three upper buttons off Bill's vest pattern. Bill never said a word about his intentions, but tied him to the corral fence and saddled up his own private horse. There were several men around camp, but they said nothing, being a party to the deal, though they noticed Bill riding away with the spoilt horse. He took him down on the creek about a mile from camp and hung him.

"How did he do it? Why, there was a big cottonwood grew on a bluff bank of the creek. One limb hung out over the bluff, over the bed of the creek. He left the running noose on the horse's neck, climbed out on this overhanging limb, taking the rope through a fork directly over the water. He then climbed down and snubbed the free end of the rope to a small tree, and began taking in his slack. When the rope began to choke the horse, he reared and plunged, throwing himself over the bluff. That settled his ever hurting anyone. He was hung higher than Haman. Bill never went back to the camp, but struck out for other quarters. There was a month's wages coming to him, but he would get that later or they might keep it. Life had charms for an old-timer like Bill, and he didn't hanker for any reputation as a broncobuster. It generally takes a verdant to pine for such honors.

"Last winter when Bill was riding the chuckline, he ran up against a new experience. It seems that some newcomer bought a range over on Black Bear. This new man sought to set at defiance the customs of the range. It was currently reported that he had refused to invite people to stay for dinner, and preferred that no one would ask for a night's lodging, even in winter. This was the gossip of the camps for miles around, so Bill and some juniper of a pardner thought they would make a call on him and see how it was. They made it a point to reach his camp shortly after noon. They met the owner just coming out of the dugout as they rode up. They exchanged the compliments of the hour, when the new man turned and locked the door of the dugout with a padlock. Bill sparred around the main question, but finally asked if it was too late to get dinner, and was very politely informed that dinner was over. This latter information was, however, qualified with a profusion of regrets. After a confession of a hard ride made that morning from a camp many miles distant, Bill asked the chance to remain overnight. Again the travelers were met with serious regrets, as no one would be at camp that night, business calling the owner away; he was just starting then. The cowman led out his horse, and after mounting and expressing for the last time his sincere regrets that he could not extend to them the hospitalities of his camp, rode away.

"Bill and his pardner moseyed in an opposite direction a short distance and held a parley. Bill was so nonplused at the reception that it took him some little time to collect his thoughts. When it thoroughly dawned on him that the courtesies of the range had been trampled underfoot by a rank newcomer and himself snubbed, he was aroused to action.

" 'Let's go back,' said Bill to his pardner, 'and at least leave our card. He might not like it if we didn't.'

"They went back and dismounted about ten steps from the door. They shot every cartridge they both had, over a hundred between them, through the door, fastened a card with their correct names on it, and rode away. One of the boys that was working there, but was absent at the time, says there was a number of canned tomato and corn crates ranked up at the rear of the dugout, in range with the door. This lad says that it looked as if they had a special grievance against those canned goods, for they were riddled with lead. That fellow lost enough by that act to have fed all the chuckline men that would bother him in a year.

"Raneka made it a rule," continued Mouse, "to go down and visit the Cheyennes every winter, sometimes staying a month. He could make a good stagger at speaking their tongue, so that together with his knowledge of the Spanish and the sign language he could converse with them readily. He was perfectly at home with them, and they all liked him. When he used to let his hair grow long, he looked like an Indian. Once, when he was wrangling horses for us during the beef-shipping season, we passed him off for an Indian on some dining-room girls.

George Wall was working with us that year, and had gone in ahead to see about the cars and find out when we could pen and the like. We had to drive to the state line, then, to ship. George took dinner at the best hotel in the town, and asked one of the dining-room girls if he might bring in an Indian to supper the next evening. They didn't know, so they referred him to the landlord. George explained to that auger, who, not wishing to offend us, consented.

"There were about ten girls in the dining room, and they were on the lookout for the Indian. The next night we penned a little before dark. Not a man would eat at the wagon; every one rode for the hotel. We fixed Bill up in fine shape, put feathers in his hair, streaked his face with red and yellow, and had him all togged out in buckskin, even to moccasins. As we entered the dining room, George led him by the hand, assuring all the girls that he was perfectly harmless. One long table accommodated us all. George, who sat at the head with our Indian on his right, begged the girls not to act as though they were afraid; he might notice it. Wall fed him pickles and lump sugar until the supper was brought on. Then he pushed back his chair about four feet, and stared at the girls like an idiot. When George ordered him to eat, he stood up at the table. When he wouldn't let him stand, he took the plate on his knee, and ate one side dish at a time. Finally, when he had eaten everything that suited his taste, he stood up and signed with his hands to the group of girls, muttering, 'Wo-haw, wo-haw.'

" 'He wants some more beef,' said Wall. 'Bring him

some more beef.' After a while he stood up and signed again, George interpreting his wants to the dining-room girls, 'Bring him some coffee. He's awful fond of coffee.'

"That supper lasted an hour, and he ate enough to kill a horse. As we left the dining room, he tried to carry away a sugar bowl, but Wall took it away from him. As we passed out George turned back and apologized to the girls, saying, 'He's a good Injun. I promised him he might eat with us. He'll talk about this for months now. When he goes back to his tribe he'll tell his squaws all about you girls feeding him.' "

Voting Bonds to the Railroad

told by
Coon Floyd

"Seems like I remember that fellow Wall," said Bradshaw, meditating.

"Why, of course you do. Weren't you with us when we voted the bonds to the railroad company?" asked Edwards.

"No, never heard of it; must have been after I left. What business did you have voting bonds?"

"Tell him, Coon. I'm too full for utterance," said Edwards.

"If you'd been in this country you'd heard of it," said Coon Floyd. "For a few years everything was dated from that event. It was like 'when the stars fell,' and 'the surrender' with the old-time darkies at home. It seems that some new line of railroad wanted to build in, and wanted bonds voted to them as bonus. Some foxy agent for this new line got among the longhorns who own the cattle on this Strip, and showed them that it was to their interest to get a competing line in the cattle traffic. The result was, these old longhorns got owly, laid their heads together, and made a little medicine. Every mother's son of us in the Strip was entitled to claim a home somewhere, so they put it up that we should come in and vote for the bonds. It was believed it would be a close race if they carried, for it was by counties that the bonds were voted. Towns that the road would run through would vote unanimously for them, but outlying towns would vote solidly against the bonds. There was a big lot of money used, wherever it came from, for we were royally entertained. Two or three days before the date set for the election, they began to head for this cow town, every man on his top horse. Everything was as free as air, and we all understood that a new railroad was a good thing for the cattle interests. We gave it not only our votes, but moral support likewise.

"It was a great gathering. The hotels fed us, and the liveries cared for our horses. The liquid refreshments were provided by the prohibition druggists of the town and were as free as the sunlight. There was an underestimate made on the amount of liquids required, for the town was dry about thirty minutes; but a regular train was run through from Wichita ahead of time, and the embarrassment overcome. There was an opposition line of railroad working against the bonds, but they didn't have any better sense than to send a man down to our town to counteract our exertions. Public sentiment was a delicate matter with us, and while this man had no influence with any of us, we didn't feel the same toward him as we might. He was distributing his tickets around, and putting up a good argument, possibly, from his point of view, when some of these old longhorns hinted to the boys to show the fellow that he wasn't wanted.

" 'Don't hurt him,' said one old cowman to this same Wall, 'but give him a scare, so he will know that we don't indorse him a little bit. Let him know that this town knows how to vote without being told. I'll send a man to rescue him, when things have gone far enough. You'll know when to let up.'

"That was sufficient. George went into a store and cut off about fifty feet of new rope. Some fellows that knew how tied a hangman's knot. As we came up to the stranger, we heard him say to a man, 'I tell you, sir, these bonds will pauperize unborn gener——' But the noose dropped over his neck, and cut short his argument. We led him a block and a half through the little town, during which there was a pointed argument between Wall and a Z Bar man whether the city scales or the stockyards arch gate would be the best place to hang him. There were a hundred men around him and hanging on to the rope, when a druggist, whom most of them knew, burst through the crowd, and whipping out a knife cut the rope within a few feet of his neck.

" 'What in hell are you varmints trying to do?' roared the druggist. 'This man is a cousin of mine. Going to hang him, are you? Well, you'll have to hang me with him when you do.'

" 'Just as soon make it two as one,' snarled George. 'When did you get the chips in this game, I'd like to know? Oppose the progress of the town, too, do you?'

" 'No, I don't,' said the druggist, 'and I'll see that my cousin here doesn't.'

" 'That's all we ask, then,' said Wall; 'turn him loose, boys. We don't want to hang no man. We hold you responsible if he opens his mouth again against the bonds.'

" 'Hold me responsible, gentlemen,' said the druggist, with a profound bow. 'Come with me, Cousin,' he said to the Anti.

"The druggist took him through his store, and up some back stairs; and once he had him alone, this was his advice, as reported to us later: 'You're a stranger to me. I lied to those men, but I saved your life. Now, I'll take you to the four o'clock train, and get you out of this town. By this act I'll incur the hatred of these people that I live amongst. So you let the idea go out that you are my cousin. Sabe? Now, stay right here and I'll bring you anything you want, but for heaven's sake, don't give me away.'

" 'Is—is—is the four o'clock train the first out?' inquired the new cousin.

" 'It is the first. I'll see you through this. I'll come up and see you every hour. Take things cool and easy now. I'm your friend, remember,' was the comfort they parted on.

"There were over seven hundred votes cast, and only one against the bonds. How that one vote got in is yet a mystery. There were no hard drinkers among the boys, all easy drinkers, men that never refused to drink. Yet voting was a little new to them, and possibly that was how this mistake occurred. We got the returns early in the evening. The county had gone by a handsome majority for the bonds. The committee on entertainment had provided a ball for us in the basement of the Opera House, it being the largest room in town. When the good news began to circulate, the merchants began building bonfires. Fellows who didn't have extra togs on for the ball got out their horses, and in squads of twenty to fifty rode through the town, painting her red. If there was one shot fired that night, there were ten thousand.

"I bought a white shirt and went to the ball. To show you how general the good feeling amongst everybody was, I squeezed the hand of an alfalfa widow during a waltz, who instantly reported the affront offered to her gallant. In her presence he took me to task for the offense. 'Young man,' said the doctor, with a quiet wink, 'this lady is under my protection. The fourteenth amendment don't apply to you nor me. Six-shooters, however, make us equal. Are you armed?'

" 'I am, sir.'

" 'Unfortunately, I am not. Will you kindly excuse me, say ten minutes?'

" 'Certainly, sir, with pleasure.'

" 'There are ladies present,' he observed. 'Let us retire.'

"On my consenting, he turned to the offended dame, and in spite of her protests and appeals to drop matters, we left the ballroom, glaring daggers at each other. Once outside, he slapped me on the back, and said, 'Say, we'll just have time to run up to my office, where I have some choice old copper-distilled, sent me by a very dear friend in Kentucky.'

"The goods were all he claimed for them, and on our return he asked me as a personal favor to apologize to the lady, admitting that he was none too solid with her himself. My doing so, he argued, would fortify him with her and wipe out rivals. The doctor was a rattling good fellow, and I'd even taken off my new shirt for him, if he'd said the word. When I made the apology, I did it on the grounds that I could not afford to have any difference, especially with a gentleman who would willingly risk his life for a lady who claimed his protection.

"No, if you never heard of voting the bonds you certainly haven't kept very close tab on affairs in this Strip. Two or three men whom I know refused to go in and vote. They ain't working in this country now. It took some of the boys ten days to go and come, but there wasn't a word said. Wages went on just the same. You ain't asleep, are you, Don Guillermo?"

"Oh, no," said Edwards with a yawn, "I feel just like

the nigger did when he eat his fill of possum, corn bread, and new molasses: pushed the platter away and said, 'Go way, 'lasses, you done los' yo sweetness.' "

Death of the Little Glassblower

told by
Billy Edwards

Bradshaw made several attempts to go, but each time some thought would enter his mind and he would return with questions about former acquaintances. Finally he inquired, "What ever became of that little fellow who was sick about your camp?"

Edwards meditated until Mouse said, "He's thinking about little St. John, the fiddler."

"Oh, yes, Patsy St. John, the little glassblower," said Edwards, as he sat up on a roll of bedding. "He's dead long ago. Died at our camp. I did something for him that I've often wondered who would do the same for me—I closed his eyes when he died. You know he came to us with the mark on his brow. There was no escape; he had consumption. He wanted to live, and struggled hard to avoid going. Until three days before his death he was hopeful; always would tell us how much better he was getting, and everyone could see that he was gradually going. We always gave him gentle horses to ride, and he would go with us on trips that we were afraid would be his last. There wasn't a man on the range who ever said 'No' to him. He was one of those little men you can't help but like; small physically, but with a heart as big as an ox's. He lived about three years on the range, was welcome wherever he went, and never made an enemy or lost a friend. He couldn't; it wasn't in him. I don't remember now how he came to the range, but think he was advised by doctors to lead an outdoor life for a change.

"He was born in the South, and was a glassblower by occupation. He would have died sooner but for his pluck and confidence that he would get well. He changed his mind one morning, lost hope that he would ever get well, and died in three days.

"It was in the spring. We were going out one morning to put in a floodgate on the river, which had washed away in a freshet. He was ready to go along. He hadn't been on a horse in two weeks. No one ever pretended to notice that he was sick. He was sensitive if you offered any sympathy, so no one offered to assist, except to saddle his horse. The old horse stood like a kitten. Not a man pretended to notice, but we all saw him put his foot in the stirrup three different times and attempt to lift himself into the saddle. He simply lacked the strength. He asked one of the boys to unsaddle the horse, saying he wouldn't go with us. Some of the boys suggested that it was a long ride, and it was best he didn't go, that we would hardly get back until after dark. But we had no idea that he was so near his end. After we left, he went back to the shack and told the cook he had changed his mind—that he was going to die.

"That night, when we came back, he was lying on his cot. We all tried to jolly him, but each got the same answer from him, 'I'm going to die.' The outfit to a man was broke up about it, but all kept up a good front. We tried to make him believe it was only one of his bad days, but he knew otherwise. He asked Joe Box and Ham Rhodes, the two biggest men in the outfit, six-footers and an inch each, to sit one on each side of his cot until he went to sleep. He knew better than any of us how near he was to crossing. But it seemed he felt safe between these two giants. We kept up a running conversation in jest with one another, though it was empty mockery. But he never pretended to notice. It was plain to us all that the fear was on him.

"We kept near the shack the next day, some of the boys always with him. The third evening he seemed to rally, talked with us all, and asked if some of the boys would not play the fiddle. He was a good player himself. Several of the boys played old favorites of his, interspersed with stories and songs, until the evening was passing pleasantly. We were recovering from our despondency with this noticeable recovery on his part, when he whispered to his two big nurses to prop him up. They did so with pillows and parkers, and he actually smiled on us all. He whispered to Joe, who in turn asked the lad sitting on the foot of the cot to play 'Farewell, My Sunny Southern Home.' Strange we had forgotten that old air—for it was a general favorite with us—and stranger now that he should ask for it. As that old familiar air was wafted out from the instrument, he raised his eyes, and seemed to wander in his mind as if trying to follow the refrain. Then something came over him, for he sat up rigid, pointing out his hand at the empty space, and muttered, 'There stands—Mother—now—under—the—oleanders. Who is—that with—her? Yes, I had—a sister. Open—the—windows. It—is—getting—dark—dark—dark.'

"Large hands laid him down tenderly, but a fit of coughing came on. He struggled in a hemorrhage for a moment, and then crossed over to the waiting figures among the oleanders. Of all the broke-up outfits, we were the most. Dead tough men bawled like babies. I had a good one myself. When we came around to our senses, we all admitted it was for the best. Since he could not get well, he was better off. We took him next day about ten miles and buried him with those freighters who were killed when the Pawnees raided this country. Some man will plant corn over their graves some day."

As Edwards finished his story, his voice trembled and

there were tears in his eyes. A strange silence had come over those gathered about the campfire. Mouse, to conceal his emotion, pretended to be asleep, while Bradshaw made an effort to clear his throat of something that would neither go up nor down, and failing in this, turned and walked away without a word. Silently we unrolled the beds, and with saddles for pillows and the dome of heaven for a roof, we fell asleep.

A Rise in the Price of Coffee

told by
Hank Blair

Among the last few herds of cattle which passed over the old Western Trail was a Running W one from southern Texas. Our outfit had overcome the obstacles incident to the barren portion of that state, and the herd had now reached the Canadian River. We were forced to make a crossing higher up that stream on account of some recent fencing near the old one. This had its advantages, as it gave us a new range and a fine camping spot. Our cattle, well watered and grazed for a few hours before night set in, showed that contentment which a well-filled stomach gives to man and beast alike.

The foreman had selected for the night a bed-ground on which the grass had not been burned that spring. This old, dry grass made a blanket over the ground, so heavy was it as it fell matted about. As it was midsummer, the elevation of this spot gave us good air. The Running W people always drove in large herds, and this one may have been a few scant of the intended thirty-five hundred. As we rounded the herd onto the spot selected, the cattle began to drop, and before we could get them into as compact a body as was desired, two thirds were lying down. We at length got them into a space of four or five acres, and the first guard having come out to take them, we rode into camp feeling assured that there would be no trouble that night. Their grunting and blowing from stomachs well filled with grass and water was a guarantee that they would rest well.

After supper we built up a big fire from driftwood and loitered around it. The fact that we had been forced to cross the river five miles higher up than in other years was looked upon as an omen that the days of the trail were nearing an end, and recollections of old times naturally followed. Finally the conversation turned to the queer people whom we had met on the range. Our foreman, Hank Blair, said he always liked to study a sheepman.

"You watch a sheepman for an hour or so," he declared, "and if he don't tip his calling by some queer act or remark, then this alkali water that I've drunk the last fifteen years has affected my reasoning. I remember once that the man I was going up the trail that year for sent me down into the lower country to receive about a hundred saddle horses which he had contracted for. I got off at a little station on the Mexican National Railway. As I strolled up into the village proper, I inquired where I could get my dinner, and was directed to the only feed trough in town. This village being two-thirds Mexican, it did not surprise me to find this *fonda* run by a greaser.

"I had barely started to eat when a man entered and sat down opposite me. His hair hadn't been cut or combed recently, and there was at least a month's stubble beard on his face. He was coatless, while the coarse overshirt which he wore was unbuttoned at the neck, revealing a faded red undershirt. He rolled his eyes cautiously as he surveyed me and the surroundings. There was nothing bad in his face, though from the first I thought I had him spotted.

"After some minutes and when the waiter had gone out of the room, he leaned partly over the table and said, whispering-like, 'Say, my friend, do you know that coffee has gone up?'

"Exercising a great deal of caution, I whispered my answer, 'No, has it?'

"Just then the waiter re-entered and he looked out of the window with an indifferent air, as though his cunning was deep and crafty, and no third person should be taken into this discovery. When the waiter went out for a few moments, we would hold little whispered conversations across the table, the subject always being *coffee.*

"Whenever the waiter was in the room we would look at each other blankly and childlike, each trying to outdo the other in guarding his secret. Dinner over, I asked him to have a cigar with me. I was grafting myself into his confidence rapidly. After he had licked his cigar all over and lighted it, we strolled out together. No other subject was discussed between us. As we walked along the street we passed a grocery store.

" 'You wait outside here,' said he, 'while I go inside and price their coffee.'

"As he came out, he gave me a cautious wink and we walked half a block before he spoke; then he said, 'They are on to the market all right; can't touch them. Let's go down to the Alliance store.' As we crossed over the street towards this store, he said to me, 'We had better not both go in.'

" 'That's a good idea,' I answered. 'You go in, for I'm not going to buy any today, but I want to help you.'

"I stayed outside while he entered the store. I was figuring how much time I could spend on this freak, when he came out. 'It's no use! It's no use! They are all on.'

" 'Oh,' I said, 'don't let's give up. There are other stores in town. Where else can we go?'

" 'We might go down to the New Orleans store, but they are Jews, and while they will pay you more for your wool, they will make it up selling you your coffee. I don't come to town but twice a year, when I sell my fall and spring clip. I range my sheep on the Arroyo Gato, sixty miles north. I work six *pastores* regular and twice as many during lambing season.'

"He talked along in this line until we reached the New Orleans store. 'You go in and get their prices,' he said. 'They know me in there, and we must not arouse any suspicion.' I went in and bought a rope I needed and incidentally priced their best coffee. When I came out I said to him, 'Bought this rope to fool them. They want twenty and a half for their best, up to a whole bag.'

" 'It's awful,' he said in reply. 'The next time coffee gets cheap, I'm going to buy enough to run me two years. I'll not get caught this way again.' He told me his wool would not be in until tomorrow, but that he liked to do his trading in advance. I finally told him that he would have to excuse me as I had quite a ride to make yet that evening. So I bade him good-by, and half an hour later having hired a horse, was tying some sailor knots on my new rope, when I saw him beckon to me from across the street. When I went over to him he said, 'Say, I just bought a whole bag. Old Juan García who runs the cash store around the corner wasn't on to the rise and I got it at twenty and a quarter. He only had the one bag but I nailed that.'

"After complimenting him on his good fortune and wishing him luck, I bade him good-by once more. As we separated he walked around a corner with a swagger, as though he had killed a sixteen-prong bull elk. As I rode out that evening I couldn't get that poor old sheepman out of my mind. The upshot of his trouble was this: the fall before when he sold his clip, coffee was likely twenty cents a pound, and now six months later it was half a cent higher. He wasn't prepared for a shock like that. It nearly upset him. But that's just like a sheepman. Since then I always notice one when I see him. Seems like long association with sheep by anyone but a Mexican just naturally saps the intellect."

"Listen!" said one of the boys.

The rich tenor voice of Sandy on herd floated out on the night air. He was singing "Nancy Lee." Across and up the river in a low ridge of sand dunes the howl of a lone gray wolf discorded with his, until both died away together.

Big Tom Plays Monte

told by
Beau

"When I was working in the Panhandle country," said Beau as he threw a dry cottonwood limb on the fire, "there drifted on to that range a fine specimen of the physical man by the name of Big Tom. We never knew any other name for him, and as everyone liked him his past was never probed into. The strange thing about him was that he couldn't ride. He was never seen on a horse.

"He was a large man, had a foot on him like a strip of breakfast bacon, and a hand like a nine-pound canvas ham. He stayed around headquarters generally, and being a good worker, always had a job. He could cut and haul more wood for ranch and branding purposes than any two men in the country. Put him in a cedar brake cutting fence posts and he was a whole outfit. Plowing fireguards in the fall, the foreman had to go out and stop him, or he would work on Sunday. Once when we had a bad prairie fire in our pasture, he threw off his hat and overshirt and for twenty-four hours fought fire until it was put out entirely. It was a picture to see his big figure loom up against a horizon of burning grass at midnight. We had to give him a wet rawhide to fight with, or he would wear out all the saddle blankets on the ranch. The fire out, he would go back to his work as though nothing had happened, while other men would be worn out for days.

"He usually took about two layoffs a year to go to town and put his wages into circulation. He was known on the range as a free, reliable drinker, and if luck came his way he could make a gambler look sick. One Christmas time a number of us went into town, and among the boys was Tom. He had about six months' wages in his pocket, a small amount of which he expected to invest in clothing, the remainder in drinks and gambling. Before we were in town half a day, sauntering around meeting acquaintances and buying little tricks we needed, one of our boys came to a couple of us where we were in a store and said, almost out of breath, 'I've been hunting you. You had better come down to this gambling joint, for Tom's got a monte game going south, and he's drinking like a fish.'

"For fear that there might be hair on the deal, we hurried around and into this joint, to see that he got a run for his money, on the square.

" 'Hello, fellows, where you been?' said he in deep guttural tones. 'I've struck an easy game here. Ah, there, you man behind the bar there. Give these boys anything they want,' said he in a commanding voice, pitching a dollar to the bartender. He had all kinds of money before him and a fat wad of bills in his pocket.

"Across the table sat the dealer, a typical frontier gambler, shuffling, stripping and riffling the deck to change the run of the cards if possible. In his face and cool gray eyes there showed no sign that either loss or gain affected him. He wouldn't even smile. Did any of you ever watch blanket Indians gamble? There's never an expression in their faces, win or lose. This dealer was a good imitation of the stoical Indian. If to lose hurt him it was not visible on the surface. Tom, though, was very talkative, boastful and defiant. The amount of drinks he had consumed served to prime him, and showed his good and evil qualities alike. He urged everyone to drink with him and was drinking himself like a cow in August.

" 'Boys, this is a square and honest game, and if it wasn't for the limit, I'd tap her for all she's worth. But they limit me, you see, so I don't get the action I want. Take down your limit, Mr. Dealer, and let's have a wide-open game," said Tom to the gambler.

" 'The limit is my protection. Cut the cards, please,' answered the gambler. Tom cut the cards and the layout fell queen-six.

" 'Ha! My old favorite, the queen!' said Tom, as he stacked up fifty dollars *alce* on his favorite card. The dealer turned the deck and the next cards fell seven-king. As Tom arranged his silver to the limit on the seven, he qualified this bet by remarking to the dealer, 'This goes *sin espadas.*' The dealer nodded and turned the deck without action. The next cards fell deuce-ace. Tom stacked his silver again to the limit on the deuce, remarking, 'In the *viejo,* Mr. Dealer. Now pull for what's in sight.'

" 'Do you want to pull?' asked the gambler.

" 'Wouldn't touch those cards for no money,' answered Tom. 'Pull yourself.' There was a craning of necks by the bystanders, a card or two fell, and they came out seven, deuce, queen. 'There now, look at that,' said Tom in disgust. 'It's too bad that an ordinary citizen like myself can't get a quiet little game out in this country to suit his tastes, and it full of gamblers, too. To sit around and pike and buck a peanut game like this makes me tired. Do you know any place that I can go and get a game to suit my tastes, Mr. Dealer?' The gambler ignored Tom's last question by asking the barkeeper to bring him the bank roll out of the safe, and a new deck of cards. He counted off the amount the game was loser on the last deal, and handed it over to Tom.

" 'Whenever I win I like to treat,' said Tom. 'What will you have, Mr. Dealer, and all you boys?'

" 'Not anything for me,' said the gambler.

" 'Ah, take a drink and be sociable,' said Tom. 'Eat, drink, and be merry, for tomorrow you may die. You better take a drink with the rest of us; it will show the proper spirit; besides, inside an hour I expect to lend you money to get your supper and breakfast with. Changing the deck won't help you, for I'll change my system.'

"The dealer shuffled. Tom gave the cards a slobbering cut with one hand, as he drained his glass with the other, wiping his chin on his sleeve. The cards fell for the layout. He put a dollar against a deuce, following it up against every favorite as they fell. That deal ended by Tom winning four or five dollars.

" 'Now, Mr. Dealer,' said Tom, 'give us a layout and if you have the nerve to take the bet, I'll tap you on the first card that falls for the contents of your roll and every sou your weasel skin contains, and stake you if I win. This game of yours hasn't life enough in it to keep me awake properly. What do you say?'

" 'You seem to be acquiring the bank roll of this game as rapidly as we care to see it change owners,' said the gambler. 'Besides, we never change our rules. Cut the cards, please.'

"The cards were cut again, and several favorite cards appearing in the layout, Tom went against them to the limit in every case. The deal ended. The gambler opened his drawer, took out his bank roll, and counting off his losses handed the sum to Tom. Folding a small bill or two that remained, he put them in his pocket, rose, tipped his chair forward, put on his coat and said, 'I'll take a drink with you, now, old sport. I'm at leisure.'

"'What do you mean—you're not quitting, I hope?' inquired Tom.

"'We'll have to play for fun if we play any longer, for you own the bank,' explained the gambler.

"'Come now,' said Tom, 'I'll treat anyhow, and buy you a bottle of champagne, if you will give me just one more layout.'

"'No, thank you, I appreciate your patronage and good fellowship better than I do your luck,' replied the gambler.

"As it dawned on Tom's befuddled mind that the game had ended for lack of funds, it was a sight to see him stow away his winnings. His pockets bulged out with silver, until he would have made a fine object lesson against the use of that metal as a circulating medium. We all took a drink at the bar together, the gambler joining in with us. This large amount of money was embarrassing to us, for it meant a long-continued debauch for Tom.

"He was so good-natured in his cups that we steered him against a clothing store for togs enough to last him a year or two. He refused to try anything on, calling for the largest in the shop in every instance. One of the boys picked out a pair of pants for him and as the universal opinion was that they would be too small, we united in urging him to try them on. There was a little side room for this purpose and into it we went. When Tom had divested himself of those he had on, he steadied himself with wonderful deliberation and tried to stand on one foot. After several attempts he succeeded in getting one leg into the new pants. But to get the second foot in was a horse of another color. After one or two attempts he gave it up. Drawing the one leg up as far as possible, he scanned it carefully and kicked it off with the remark to the clerk, 'Wrap them up, she's a fit.'

"This freak of the plains spent and played his money as freely as though it were gravel that could be picked up in the bed of the creek. For the time being we were his enforced guests, and he was a host such as you read about: 'His hospitality knew no bounds and his jug had no bottom.' I remember we told him about some fine Mackinaw blankets that we had seen at a store lower down the street. He went with us, buying a whole dozen and presenting each one of us with a fine blanket. When he produced his money to pay, he emptied his pockets on the counter and authorized the merchant 'to cut out what he wanted.'

"At the time we entered this store, it being after dark, the merchant was waiting on an elderly stoop-shouldered woman. After making a few small purchases of the staples of life, she passed out, when it only took Tom a moment to decide on buying the dozen blankets. As each of us was selecting our blanket, the colors variegating, the merchant in a social spirit inquired, 'Did none of you boys know that old lady I was trading with when you came in? Why, that was Frank Traylor's mother.'

"Tom sobered in an instant. 'You don't mean to say that that old lady is the mother of Frank Traylor who was killed by a horse at our ranch?' he inquired. The merchant reaffirmed the statement.

" 'Frank Traylor's mother!' repeated Tom. 'Poor old woman! Why, I sat night and day by Frank's bedside after the accident until he died. And that old lady was Frank Traylor's mother!'

"It was plain to be seen that Tom was moved beyond the ordinary. He was for following her at once. But the old woman had passed out of sight, darkness having swallowed up all trace of her. We returned to our hotel with the blankets, and to our surprise, Tom proposed retiring instead of making a night of it as usual when drinking. My chum and I had a room next to Tom's, and all during the night we could hear him rummaging around. We slept late the next morning and were awakened by Tom bursting into our room, smiling and sober.

" 'Get up, fellows,' said he. 'I'm busted and we're going home today. And you can just bet Mrs. Traylor will have plenty of provisions and blankets this winter. No, I didn't see her but I fixed it with the merchant. Get up, you lazy varmints.' "

How Doc Langford Got His Nickname

told by
Bold Richard

"What horse is that nickering?" asked the foreman, as he raised his head from a saddle and peered out into the darkness.

"Oh, it's that old flea-bit night horse of mine," said Beau. "He's out there on picket and has just missed his pal that Sandy is now riding on herd. He's plenty old enough not to fret, but he will."

As the horse quieted down, a fellow by the name of

How Doc Langford Got His Nickname

Bold Richard asked, "Did I ever tell you about Doc Langford and how he got the name?"

"No," said the foreman, "what about him?"

"Well, I went up the trail a few years ago with a Three Circle herd of cattle which we delivered in the Strip. We turned the herd loose in a through pasture early in the year, and the foreman on that range offered me a job, so I went to work for him. About two years afterward the original Oklahoma opened, and as it was early in the spring with nothing to do, a number of us rode down there. We were simply spectators and we took in everything. There was a great deal of fun around and some seriousness. We made a rush with the rest when the word was given, for probably a mile, just to try our horses. None of us wanted claims, so after the first dash out of the box, we turned and rode back leisurely.

"The abandoned camp looked as desolate as a bird's nest in winter. Here and there a tent and a few covered wagons showed that it was not entirely deserted. As we were looking over the deserted place, a little girl ran out of one of the tents and skipped right over the ground to us as we sat on our horses. She asked breathlessly, 'Is any of you gentlemen a doctor or a married man?'

"The question stunned most of us, but Langford answered instantly, 'Yes, I'm a doctor and a married man besides. What can I do for you, little girl?'

" 'There's a woman down in that tent, sir. She's very sick, and she said if any of you was a doctor or a married man to come down.'

"Langford dismounted from his horse, handing the reins to one of the boys, took the child by the hand and the two were soon out of sight in the tent. We were struck in a quarter so sudden and unexpected that we sat around on our horses trying to make it out. But never a one of us guessed the real trouble. We could see Langford with his coat off, going in and out, heating water and flying around free and lively. The little girl went down the creek to another tent, and presently returned, a woman with her. We thought that Langford would come back to us then, but he didn't. It was growing late in the day, and we had a long ride to make. We began to get uneasy, but Langford never showed up. None of us would go near the sick woman for we felt it would be an intrusion, and as he was the only married one in the crowd, possibly we wouldn't be wanted. We had dismounted and were lying around, patiently waiting for him. He was gone over two hours, when he came out, putting on his coat as he walked. When he was within hailing distance, he stopped and called, 'Some of you citizens bring the doctor his horse.' As we all went up to him he said, 'Address me in my professional capacity, please. There is a boy baby down at the tent as big as a yearling; mother and child doing well.'

"We looked at each other in mutual astonishment when this truth dawned on us. As it was late, we mounted our horses and hit the trail for camp. We tried to ride as near Langford as possible, in order to hear him give his experience. But he frowned on us, remarking, 'It looks like vulgar varmints of your calling would show some respect for a professional man like myself by keeping a respectful distance.' When he had played this role long enough, he turned halfway in his saddle and said, 'The best thing that happened was when I was bandaging the baby, having torn up its papa's Sunday shirt for the purpose. I turned to the woman who was assisting me, and assuming that professional air which has carried the medical fraternity through many a trying ordeal, I asked her, "Madam, what style of navel do you like best? Now, I can cut this one so it will grow either pouched or caved—either style you prefer."'

"'Isn't he a rotten liar?' said one of the boys.

"'That's right, dispute with the doctor,' protested he, with an air of injured innocence.

"I worked on that range several years after that and the name of Doc always clung to him."

A Jagger from Jaggertown

told by
Hank Blair's Wrangler

"Don't put any more wood on the fire," said the foreman. "We'll be turning in soon."

"I just want to make those fellows on herd think we are having a big time," said the horse wrangler, as he threw down an armful of wood.

"But we can't sleep with too much light," said Blair. "You are not like a chap who went over this very same trail, who used to say that he didn't care if he slept or not, as he wasn't paid for sleeping," replied the wrangler.

"Who was that?" inquired the foreman.

"They called him the Professor," said the wrangler.

"Tell us about him," said one of the boys.

"I have missed him the last few years," said the wrangler, who was the oldest man amongst us, and in his younger days had sailed on the high seas, "but he was a character in his time, and was known from the headwaters of the Missouri to the mouth of the Rio Grande. He was a Scotchman, a younger son or something like that; drifted onto the range from Canada, I think. He never aired his grievances against the social customs of his native land, but little things would creep out. His older brother at home was a titled gentleman, though he never told us this directly.

"When I was twenty, I thought my education was fair, but in the presence of the Professor I knew enough to feel that I knew nothing. In intelligence he was a giant. He might have graced the faculty of any college with credit to it and himself. What brought him to this low level was plain; he was a boozer from Boozerville, a jagger from Jaggertown. He was so abandoned to the habit that he often wished that he might never have a dollar if booze was to be had. He was a complex man with wide extremes. Without apology, he always acknowledged his responsibility to his Creator. Possibly this was due to his early training. He was harmless, though everyone feared him. In conversation he was delightful, but in an argument he would humble to the dust anyone who dared to cross swords with him. In an intellectual set-to, the egotism of many an opponent suffered. The only evidence that he possessed affection was shown by his love for horses. He neither cultivated nor encouraged human friendship. In thought he followed no man; in all other things he was obedient.

"He had voluntarily chosen the life he led. Once north of here, higher up the trail, he got too close to whiskey and it wasn't long before he rode back and asked the cook to let him drive the wagon. They changed places and before he drove a mile, the fore wheel dropped into a rut and he dove over the dashboard. He realized his danger sufficiently to grab a mule by a hind leg, cling to it for dear life, hollowing, 'Whoa!' The horse wrangler saw the accident and went to his assistance. When the Professor crawled out from under the wagon he was a soberer man. This same mule had kicked many a sober man, and why he didn't kill him is a mystery.

"The result of one of these periodicals was a long spell of sickness. It occurred in a Western frontier town where he was a stranger, moneyless and apparently friendless. A physician who waited on him asked him in one of his rational moments if he had any friends whom he wished to acquaint with his condition. He gave the physician his name, possibly the first time it ever was known, and the name of a Masonic lodge in Canada, and asked that they be wired of his plight. Word came back to give him the best attention procurable and to present all bills to them. He recovered and went his way, being soon forgotten by those who knew of this illness. It was then that a little of his past life came to the surface. In sickness or accident, he was always mysteriously cared for.

"The stars were an alphabet to him. He could point out stars to us and name them as readily as he could his own mount of horses. He could tell us the names of astronomers who first gave us a history of this or that star. He always asked for third guard on night herd, claiming that night was time for meditation. 'When night lets down her curtain and pins it with a star' and 'Leave the world to darkness and to me' were favorite quotations of his.

"Many a little oration did he deliver us. One commenced this way: 'Last night as I rode around the sleeping cattle, I thought if the poor Indian could see God in the clouds and hear him in the winds, why should not I, who have had all the advantages that the civilization of the world before me has to offer, see in that North Star and the constellations that surround it the handiwork of a Divine Creator. That same power which fixes one stationary and give their laws to the moving ones, has not forgotten a worthless wretch like myself, but has implanted a hope and provided a way whereby I may rise to things higher.' He could never understand, he said, why God in His wisdom had gifted him for a higher life and had permitted him to sink so low, besides cursing him with a full knowledge of his own degradation.

"But there was only one end for him—the grave, and that more than likely in the potter's field. He seemed like a water-logged derelict at sea, floating listlessly in the roll of ocean. Far from land, rudderless, helpless, abandoned! He reminded me of a wrecked East Indiaman, grand in its silent desolation, in mid-ocean. Night after night he rode his own chosen hours of darkness, all alone, 'grand, gloomy, and peculiar,' a giant in intellect, but a wreck, aimless, hopeless, and rudderless, with no compass to guide him in this world's raging seas."

This vivid and tragic delineation of the Professor by the wrangler affected no one, as we had all seen similar characters time and again. The plains, like a great city, have their flotsam and jetsam of human wrecks. The boys unrolled their blankets for the night, the fire flickered low, the second guard brought in their horses from picket and stood round the smoldering fire, sipping coffee and rolling cigarettes, and sleep settled over all—save the guard.

Cow Coroner for the Sap

told by
Red Earnest

Our acquaintance began at Doan's Store in '83. The Red River had been on a rampage for a week, and twenty trail herds lay water-bound around the old ford. Just why I should have singled out "Red" Earnest from among three hundred other men who comprised the different cow outfits, and why we should have become lifelong friends, is not as clear as it might be. Earnest was a trail boss at the time and I was nothing but a common cowhand, making my second trip with Don Lovell's cattle to an Indian agency in Dakota. It must have been his musical voice, his languid manner, and his superior horsemanship that attracted me, for he was anything but handsome. My good opinion of old Red was strengthened when the river fell enough for us to ferry the wagons over and he was elected captain over the outfits in swimming the herds. I remember the ease with which, under his direction, we swam sixty-five thousand cattle across Red River between the morning hours and sunset. And during that day's work he did not issue a direct order, mere suggestion being sufficient, yet every man knew that it was a master hand that selected the entrance, that foresaw the landing on the farther bank, sent one herd on its way and summoned another to its struggle with the receding torrent.

We met again the same summer at Ogallala on the Platte. As the succeeding years passed, the bond between us strengthened like a hand-forged chain, every link tested in a comradeship and every one ringing true as a fresh-minted coin. Then the trail ended and we drifted apart, Red to railroading in Mexico, while I followed mining camps from Cripple Creek to the Klondike and back to the Thunder Mountain excitement. Years passed without even the exchange of a letter, when circumstances again threw us together, the old bond seemingly as strong as ever, not a rusty link in the chain. Red had quit Mexico, had held a position of trust with a railroad in Texas, and at the time of our reunion was in the customs service of Uncle Sam on the Rio Grande. Being a man of domestic tastes, he had married and surrounded himself by a family, and when I insisted that he must spend his next vacation with me in Colorado, he looked appealingly at his wife and children as if to ask whether he might go. Unfortunately I had no home or the invitation would have included the family, but with none to entertain but old Red all I would need was the shade of a pine tree and a blanket. The plains, over which both of us had trailed cattle, were no longer ours, but the solitude of the mountains still possessed a charm and I planned to give my old friend an outing in the Rockies.

"I'll try to arrange it," was the promise Red made me.

In company with congenial friends I had hunted for several seasons on the Flat Top Mountains in my adopted state. One of our regular party had married the winter before and dropped out from our number; when I proposed my old friend Earnest for the vacancy and vouched for his comradeship, he was accepted. Now that there were people to observe them, laws had been enacted, and we accordingly made preparations to hunt during the open season. My Texas friend arrived on time, saddle and pack horses were secured at the railroad destination, and with our own accouterments and camp equipage, a party of four of us took up the trail for the Flat Tops. Neither guide, packer, nor cook was needed, and old Red even showed me a new way to throw a lash rope in packing, then in use among the Rangers and river guards along the Rio Grande.

Up, up the mountain we trailed, leaving the haunts of civilization far behind, halting on the banks of Trapper's Lake for a few days' trout fishing, then away for our old camp at the foot of Sleepy Cat. The latter mountain bared its head above timber line, while its base was interspersed with open parks and thickety pine forest—an ideal summer range for black-tail deer. Since early morning the pack train had toiled up the mountainside, halting for blowing spells and starting again in unison without a word of command. Once, when crossing a rivulet, we noticed the fresh tracks of a cub bear, even where bruin had puddled the eddy water, and again where one had broken down an alder bush and made a dinner from its berries. It was the middle of the afternoon when the final camp was reached, the packs unlashed, the saddle horses freed, with nothing but a tinkling bell to encumber their freedom. While one man built a fire, another sliced the bacon, a third made the biscuit, and I put on the coffeepot to boil, and with sharp appetites the four of us sat down to a satisfying meal. As we expected to remain at this camp some three weeks, we lost no time in setting the camp in order before nightfall. Young pines were cut, two small tents were floored with boughs until their interiors were like a mattress and reeked with the resinous odors of balsam and fir. Dead trees were felled for wood, and as the shadows of night lowered around us, everything was secure against surprise of storm or changing weather.

As the elevation was chilly, we built up a roaring fire of dry pine logs and lounged around it, recalling old times around other campfires, in other days, in other climes. Both of the other men had regaled us with stories of prospecting, of wonderful strikes in mother lodes, of placers that ran a dollar to the pan. I had exhausted my stock of cattle and Western experiences without provoking a comment from the languid Texan who lounged on the opposite side of the fire. The hour grew late, the other two men retired to their tent, and still Red Earnest lay on his side, peering into the fire which sputtered and murmured on, singing its own song. Several times I was on the point of suggesting our blankets, when Red lifted his head from his open palm, and sitting up Indian fashion, asked me if I had ever heard any of his experiences when he was claim agent of the San Antonio and Aransas Pass Railway. Possibly there was a story in the query, and I grunted encouragement by a negative answer, and otherwise manifested interest. Red rolled a cigarette, lighted it with a brand, poked the fire, resumed his recumbent position, and began.

"Let's see; you say you were mining in Cripple Creek in '91? Yes, that's right; it was in '92 that I left Mexico to accept the position of claim agent on the Sap. I was bossing a grading gang out on the front, when the Aransas Pass people began to skirmish around for a practical cowman to act as claim agent for their line. The road was a new one at the time, the right-of-way was unfenced, while the line ran nearly its entire mileage through pastures. The result was that scarcely a day passed but from one to a dozen claims were filed against the company for cattle killed by its trains. Captain Kenedy, of the Laurel Leaf ranch, was one of the promoters of the Sap, and in looking over an annual statement, he noticed that the company was paying about double the actual value of all cattle killed by its lines. The road was struggling for its existence, and something had to be done to check the extravagance in allowing these claims for killed and injured cattle.

"I had driven half a dozen trail herds for Captain Kenedy, and when the Sap officials decided to employ a practical man in their claim department, my old employer fairly burnt the wires in locating me. On receipt of his message I had no idea what was wanted, but I'd have circled the earth on a word from the old Captain. Well, it didn't take me very long to sever the ties that bound me over a hundred greasers, and report to my old employer. I had hopes it was some big cattle deal that had called me north of the Rio Grande, but instead it was that measly job of claim agent, commonly called "cow coroner." The old Captain took me under his wing at once, and informed me that every old lank dun cow killed on the line, after her remains were burned or buried, turned out to be a purebred Shorthorn or an imported Hereford. He assured me that the company was being robbed, and insisted that I take the position as a personal favor to him, at least until the prevailing practice was broken up, when all obligation might cease at my pleasure.

"I don't mind telling you that I was engaged to my future wife at the time. Her folks lived in a little town on one of the branch lines, and with a pass in my pocket I took to white shirts and traveled extensively. Within a month after I took the job, the price of cattle killed along the lines went down to current figures—they simply had to show me their improved stock. In a little while I knew every brand on the lines and adjusted the claims from the office at headquarters. It seemed as if the cows quit sleeping on the grade, business dropped off to nothing, and I was on the point of thinking that my work was done, when I ran up against a professional case.

"I had just been married and was anxious to make a reputation with the company, when a claim came in for a stallion killed on the Gulf line. The injured party very modestly sent in his bill for a thousand dollars, referred to his neighbors as witnesses to the value of the animal, and assured us that the loss was one that no recompense could wholly alleviate. There was an air of sincerity in the attached letter that was convincing, and the claim being an unusually large one, I concluded to run down the road and give the matter my personal attention. I even visited the spot—of course a week afterward—saw the newly made equine grave by the roadside, interviewed the section foreman and his crew, secured all the details and called on the claimant. According to his story the poor fellow was simply ruined, and from his pitiful recital even my sympathy was moved. The neighbors vouched for the horse and his value, everything seemed perfectly natural, and I was at my wit's end. The owner had returned from a distant ranch, had left the stallion safely in his stall at nine o'clock at night, but in some unexplainable manner the horse had slipped his halter, made his escape from the stable, and the next morning was found, mangled almost beyond recognition, on our right-of-way. The manner of death was conclusive, the section men, acting under general orders, had promptly buried the remains, and it only remained for the company to satisfy the owner for his loss.

"Railroads are inclined to be dilatory in settling such claims, and I took my time before adjusting the account. A week passed, when I received a call from the claimant. When I suggested a compromise there was a decided change in his tone, his grief having changed to defiance, and he very curtly informed he that I might either settle then or he would leave the account with attorneys for collecton. He wasted no words with me, in fact, overplayed the part, and I became suspicious of him. Had he maintained a heartbroken attitude, as when I first met him, my suspicions might not have been aroused by his studied acting of the second role. The company retained a firm of lawyers by the year, and in parting with my caller I met his bravado by inviting him to bring suit without loss of time. I was bluffing with a four-flush hand myself, for I had not an iota of evidence that anything was irregular, but concluded to play my cards just as if I held four aces. Within a week attorneys notified me that unless I settled their client's claim for a stallion killed on our right-of-way, they would be compelled to file a suit for the damages claimed. I answered them promptly, assuring them that there was no occasion to wait ten days, but to bring their suit at once. Tom, did you ever believe a thing just a little stronger than the evidence justified? Well, that was the situation I was in; something told me that that claimant was a rascal and it was up to me to prove him one.

"Expecting a suit to be filed, I went back to the scene of the killing and spent a day in again going over the details. Only a few new facts of any possible value were unearthed, one that the horse had been killed by a southbound train (at least there were indications to that effect) and that the claimant had only lived there for a period of two months before the accident and that he had since taken his departure for good. Every effort to locate the previous residence of the horse's owner proved futile, while the good name he bore among the neighbors was simply discouraging. I returned to headquarters in San Antonio, got out the train sheets for the night on which the stallion was killed, examined every conductor's and engineer's report who had passed over the line on that date, without finding a mention of having struck an animal. The reports showed that the road had handled six trains of cattle out of Alice that night for the Indian Territory, the engines and cabooses going south on a clear track, passing the point where the horse was killed between ten o'clock and midnight. Returning with the cattle, the trains had passed the nearest station to the scene of the accident between the hours of four and seven in the morning, at which latter hour the mangled remains of the stallion were found by the section crew. I personally interviewed every one of the twelve engineers and firemen, and none had any recollection of striking an animal on the curve below Normanna. A horse usually sleeps standing, and how one could be killed without attracting the attention of anyone, or the shock being felt on the engine, was a mystery to me.

"My superiors counseled a compromise, yet I had an

intuition that I was on the right track and I was hopeful that something would turn up in my favor. The lawyers for the claimant failed to file their suit at the expiration of the given limit, and I even accepted that as a weakness of their claim. In fact, I was clinging to straws for evidence, as I did not have a plausible reason on which to fight the case. A consultation was agreed on; the claimant was absent and his attorneys held out for the full amount, the result being nothing but a war of words, threats, and recriminations.

"Still the suit was not filed, and to keep such matters pending is a railroad's long suit. It was the other fellow that was worrying, and after a few months had elapsed, a conciliatory proposition again reached me from the law firm, offering to renew the consultation, looking to a compromise. Still four-flushing, I declined the conference and once more invited them to file their suit. The absence of the claimant was a straw in our favor, and I was quite willing to have him come into court, where his prior record as a good citizen might be established. At least it would afford an opportunity to put our detectives on his trail and unearth his antecedents, as he had simply dropped out of sight for the present.

"It was six months before the suit was finally filed. Our reply consisted of generalities and denying the value of the horse, as we had neither evidence nor defensible ground on which to make a fight. Court only met twice a year in Bee County, and before the date set for trial, overtures were again made looking to a settlement without recourse to law. I gave the proposal a stony reply, assuring counsel for the claimant that we were all ready for the trial and trusted there would be no delay on their part. At this juncture my superiors took a hand, insisting that the time was ripe for a compromise, and urged my securing a definite proposition from the plaintiff's attorneys. The company's lawyers advised the same course, and I yielded only so far as sending our counsel to hold a conference, with the distinct understanding that any agreement must have my approval to make it final. My belief that the plaintiff was a rascal was never shaken for a moment, yet he was so smooth and systematic that I could not pick a flaw in his work. There were an abundance of suspicious circumstances but none of them strong enough for a successful defense, while the fact was beyond dispute that a stallion had been killed on our right-of-way, buried by our own section men, and was then rotting in his grave.

"The conference resulted in an offer of settlement in consideration of seven hundred and fifty dollars. My superiors and counsel for the company urged its acceptance, but I stood alone and fought them to the last ditch. Threats of my dismissal were even made, but I rallied Captain Kenedy, one of the directors of the road, to my backing. The old Captain and I had been through several tight places in cattle, always coming out on top, and with my old employer patting me on the back I rounded up the big augers at headquarters. I talked so straight to them that they understood that sitting down on me meant defying one of the directors of the road, an old cowman whose influence in securing cattle traffic was worth more than any half-dozen men connected with the line. They came back at me with the argument that our defense was lame, that we did not have a leg to stand on, and that a trial meant a verdict in full with costs added. I stood out for making no concession until every doubt was cleared up, and urged that nothing but a trial would remove my suspicions. As a final compromise among ourselves, it was agreed to let the issue come to a hearing, when to the surprise of everyone at headquarters but me a continuance was asked for by the plaintiff's attorneys. Their client had met with an accident, was in a hospital with a broken leg; our counsel winked acquiescence, and the case went over until the next term of court.

"It was my inning now. I threw the gaffs into my superiors at headquarters, and they took off their hats to me over the outcome of our first attempt at a trial. Before the next term of court came around, half a dozen propositions were made to settle, but I spurned them all, and insisted on the plaintiff establishing his claim before a regular tribunal of justice. Within a month of the date set for the second trial, a compromise was offered for five hundred dollars and again refused. In the interim between courts we were unable to gather a single fact that threw any light on our side, the whereabouts of the plaintiff was still unknown to us, yet we prepared to bring the matter to a hearing or demand a dismissal of the case.

"It lacked about a week of the fixed date, when one morning as I looked over the *San Antonio Express* my attention was attracted by the arrest of a party in the interior of the state for defrauding the Gulf, Colorado and Santa Fe Railroad out of twelve hundred dollars.

The money had been secured in payment for a valuable Kentucky jack, supposed to have been killed by a train, but two years afterward the animal was found alive and well by a detective in the employ of the railroad company, and hence the arrest. There was a similarity in names between the party in detention and the gentleman who had a thousand-dollar stallion killed on our line. I took the first train out of town for the scene, readily identified the prisoner as the plaintiff against the Sap, and the long-looked-for light began to shine. His home was easily located, and the next day I had the pleasure of seeing the stallion, supposed to have been killed on our road, a beauty and worth every dollar claimed. I came back with a high card up my sleeve, received the congratulations of my superiors, who raised my salary on the spot. The crook had simply substituted for the valuable one some old worthless horse, killed and mutilated him, while a confederate had done the vanishing trick with the real one. Simple as sucking eggs. Let's turn in."

We arose from the fire, listened a moment to the tinkling of the bell, and as we entered the tent I inquired why my old friend had left the employ of the railroad.

"Well, Quirk," said he, "Captain Kenedy died, the company fenced the right-of-way, the position degenerated into an office job, and I ain't used to anything like that. The government needed some river guards, the position of mounted inspector was offered me, and I always like to quit a job while my reputation's good."

The fire shone through the canvas, dimly lighting up

the interior of the tent, the resinous odors from the pine boughs lulled us into drowsiness, and we fell asleep to dream of cub bear tracks and six-prong bucks breaking from cover.